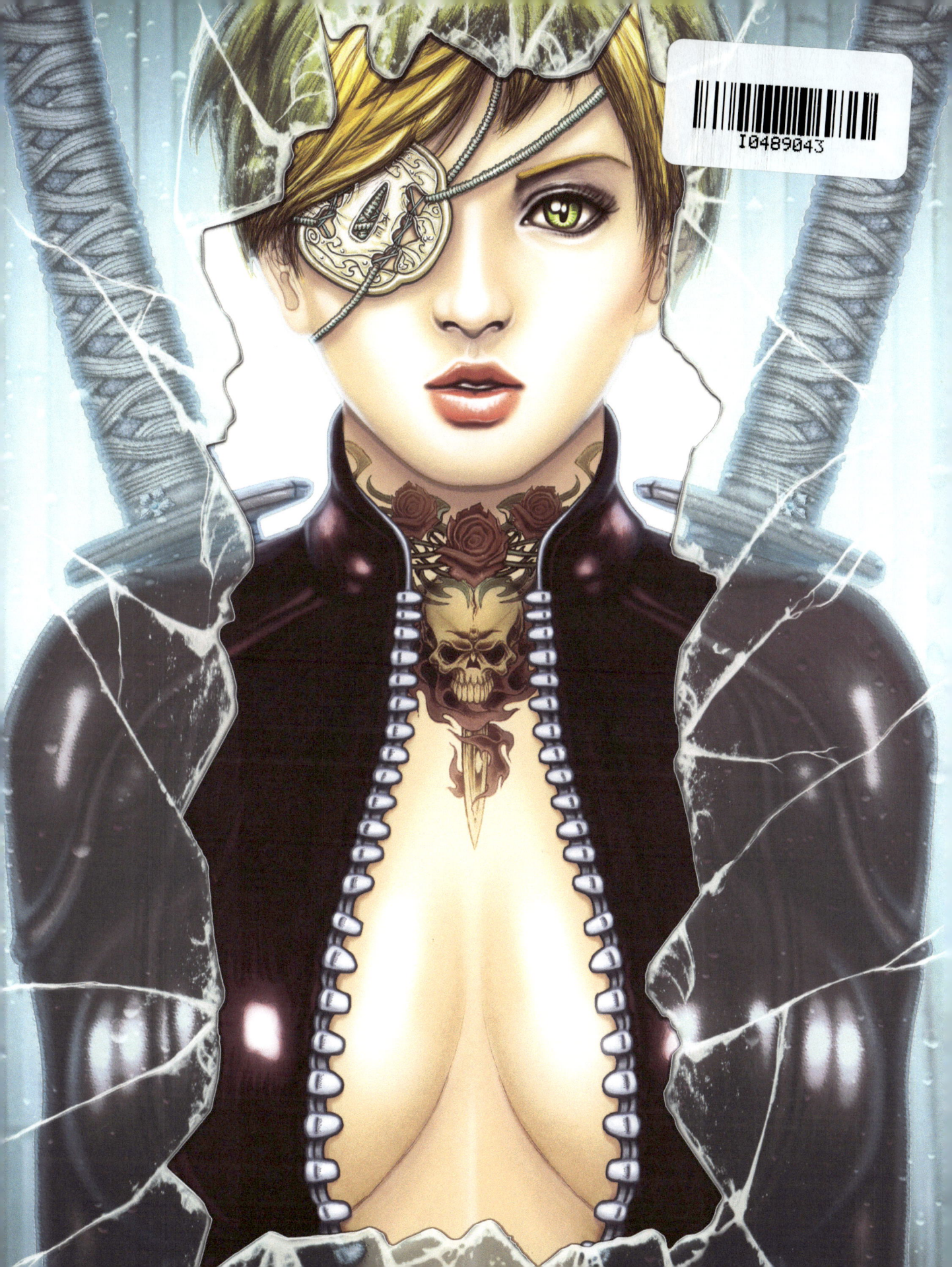

I0489043

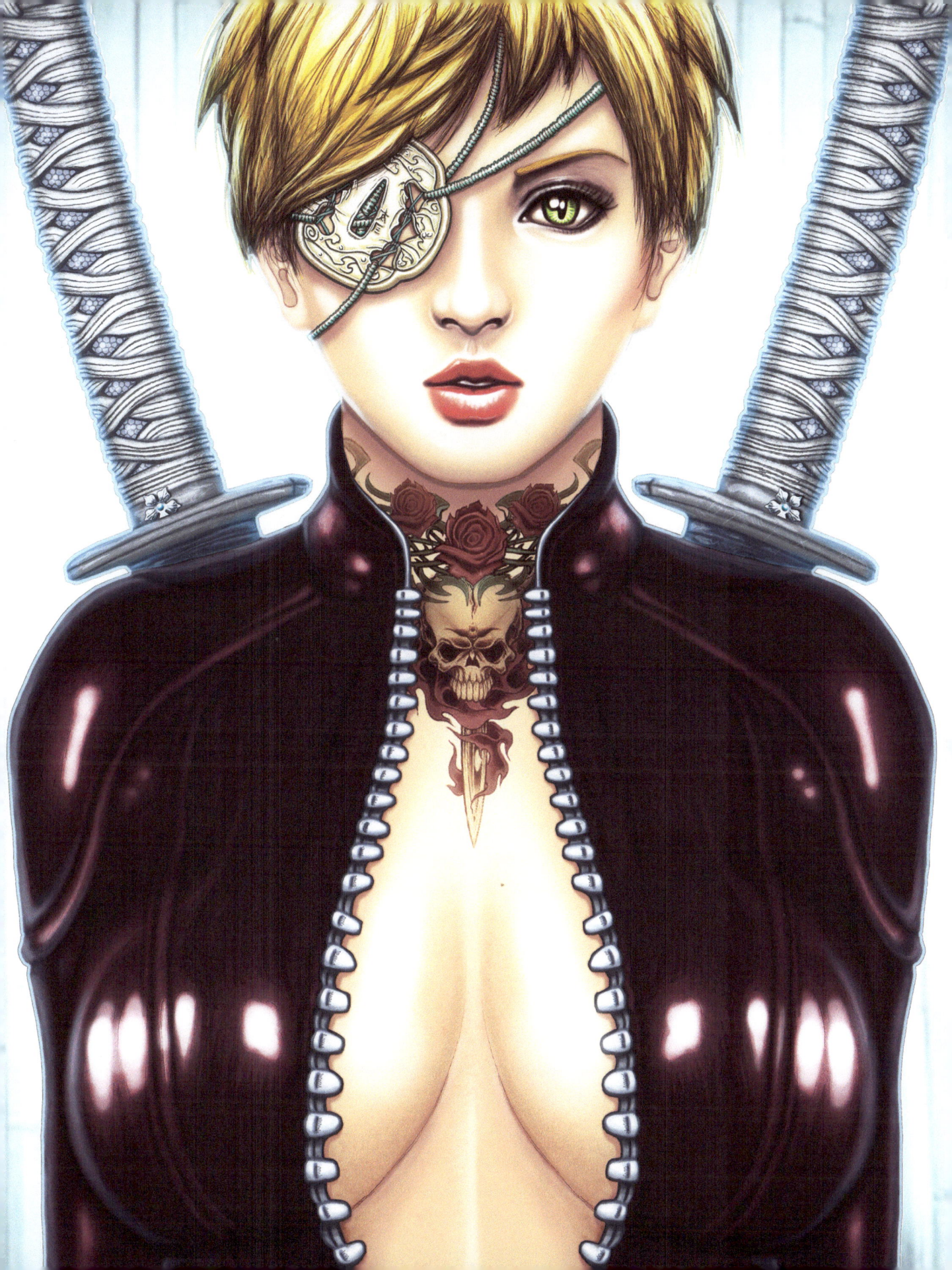

THE ART OF
ALFREDO CACCAMO

MINI-ARTBOOK - 2014

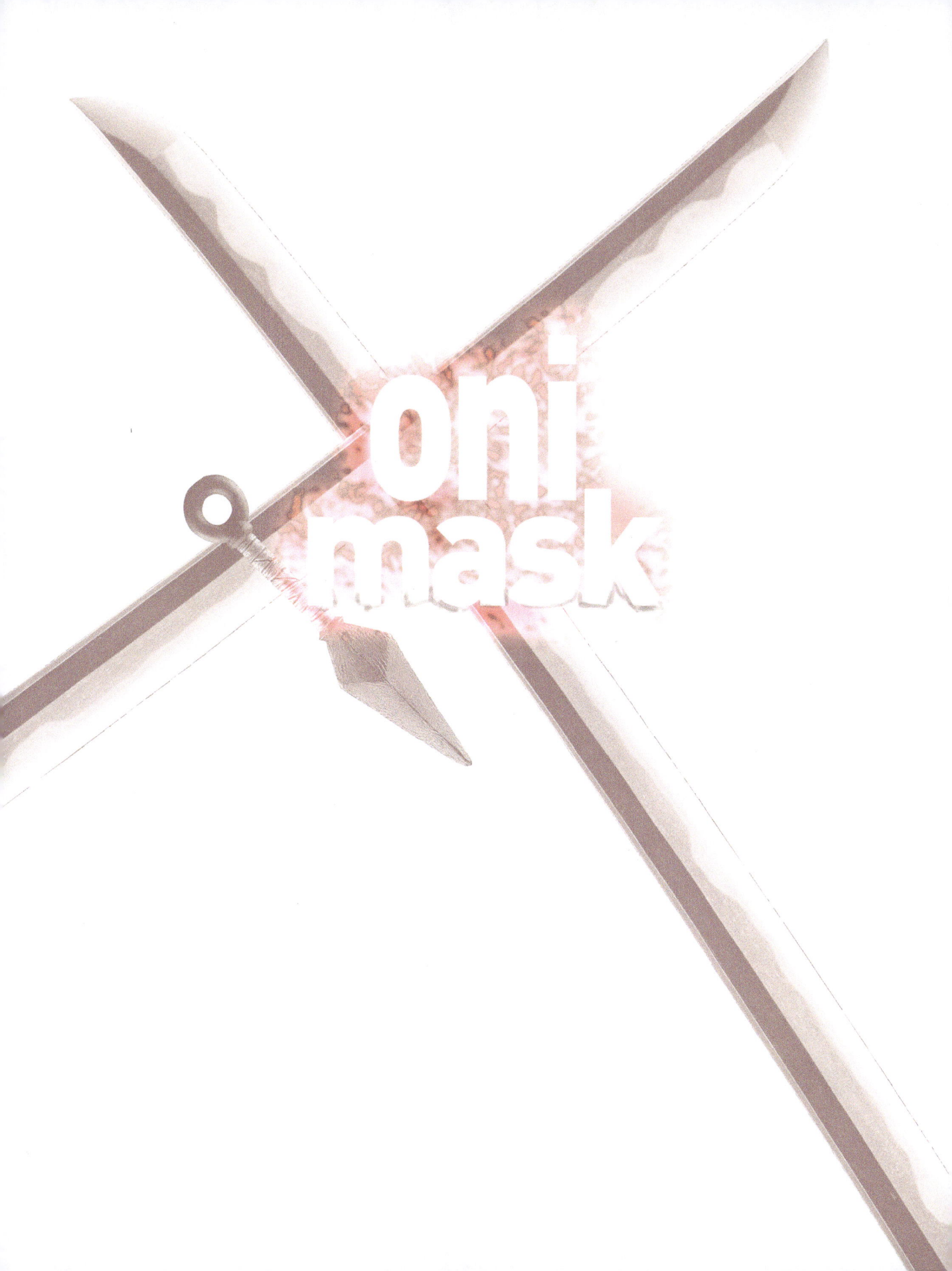

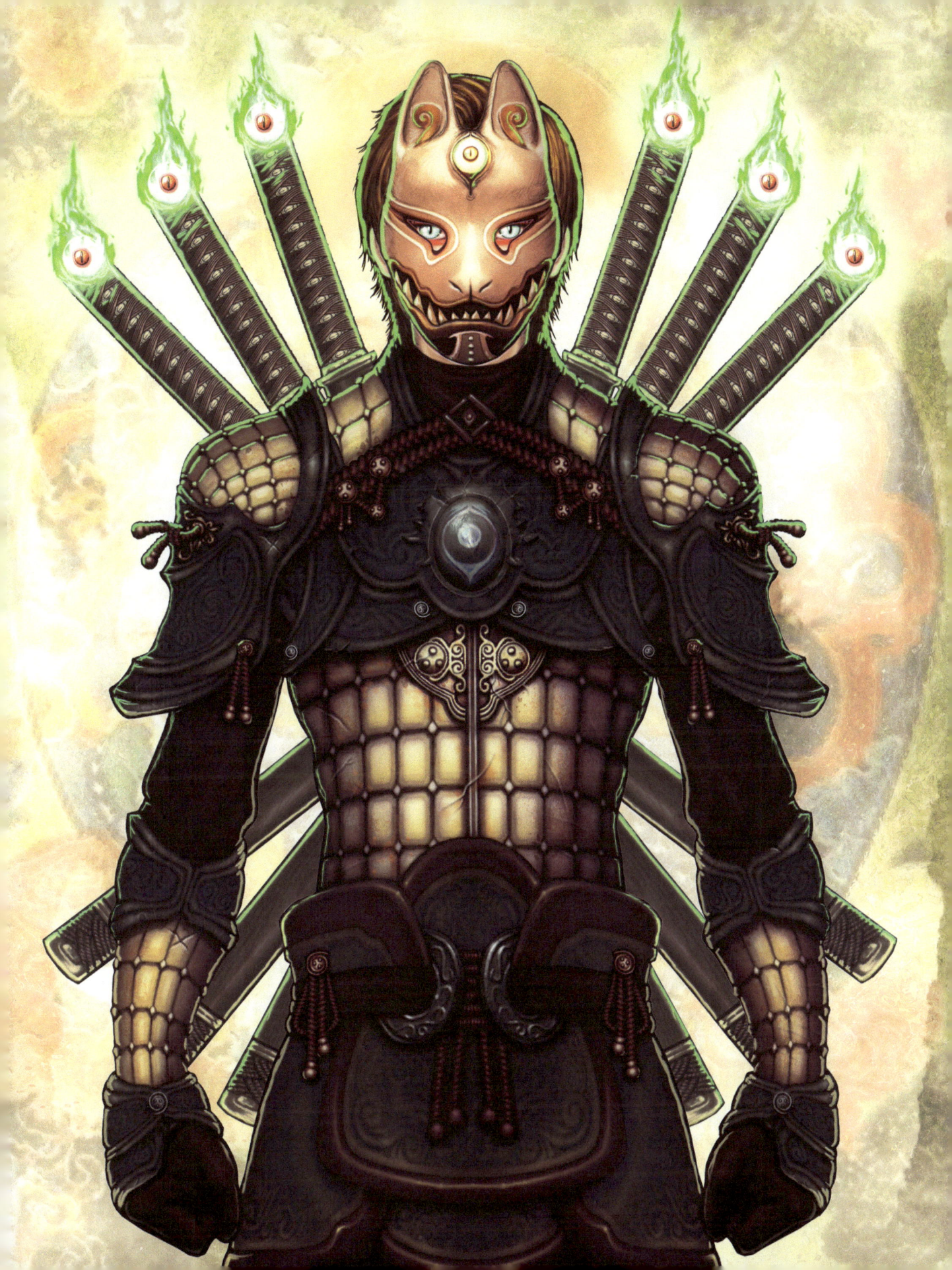

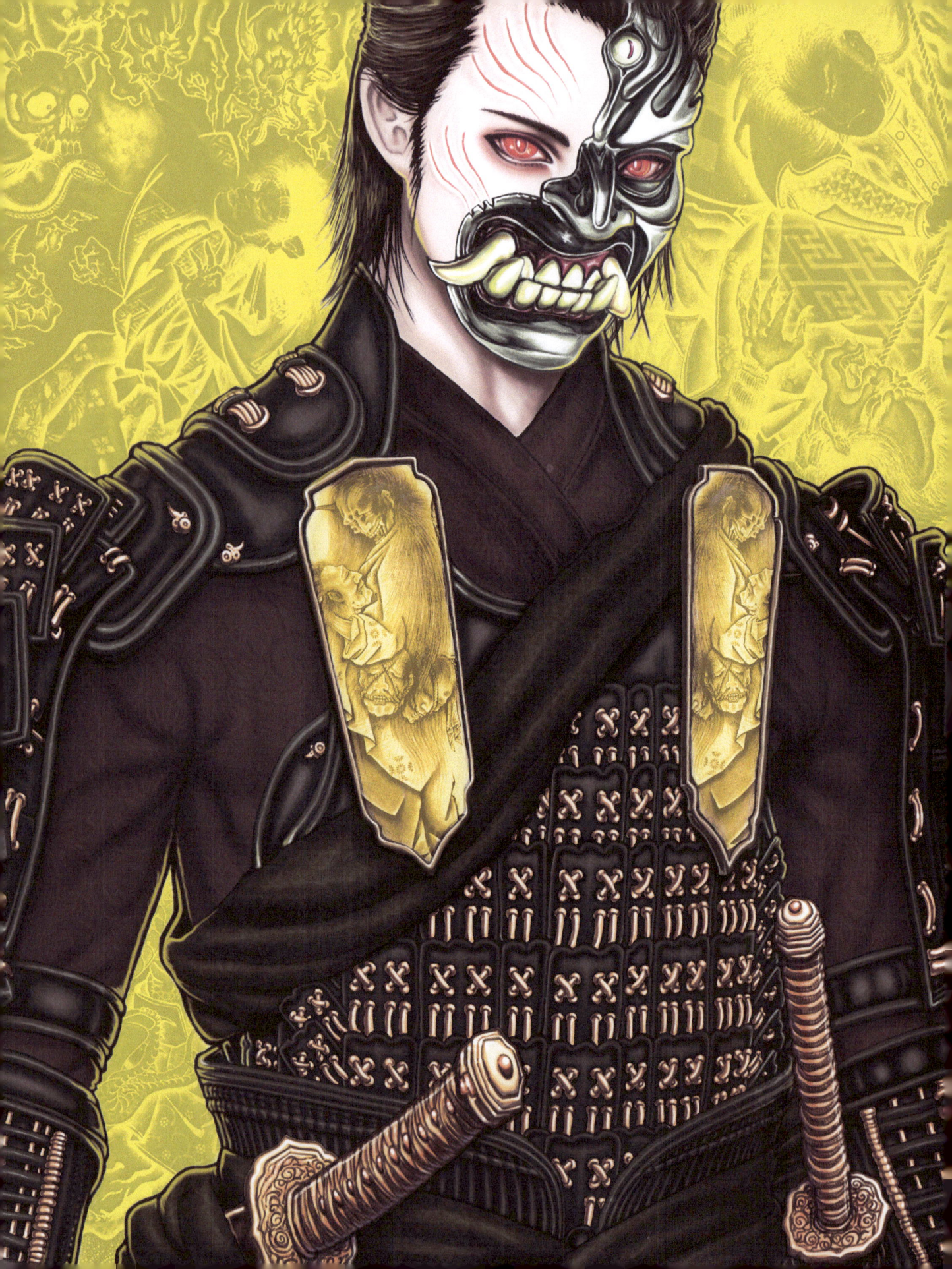

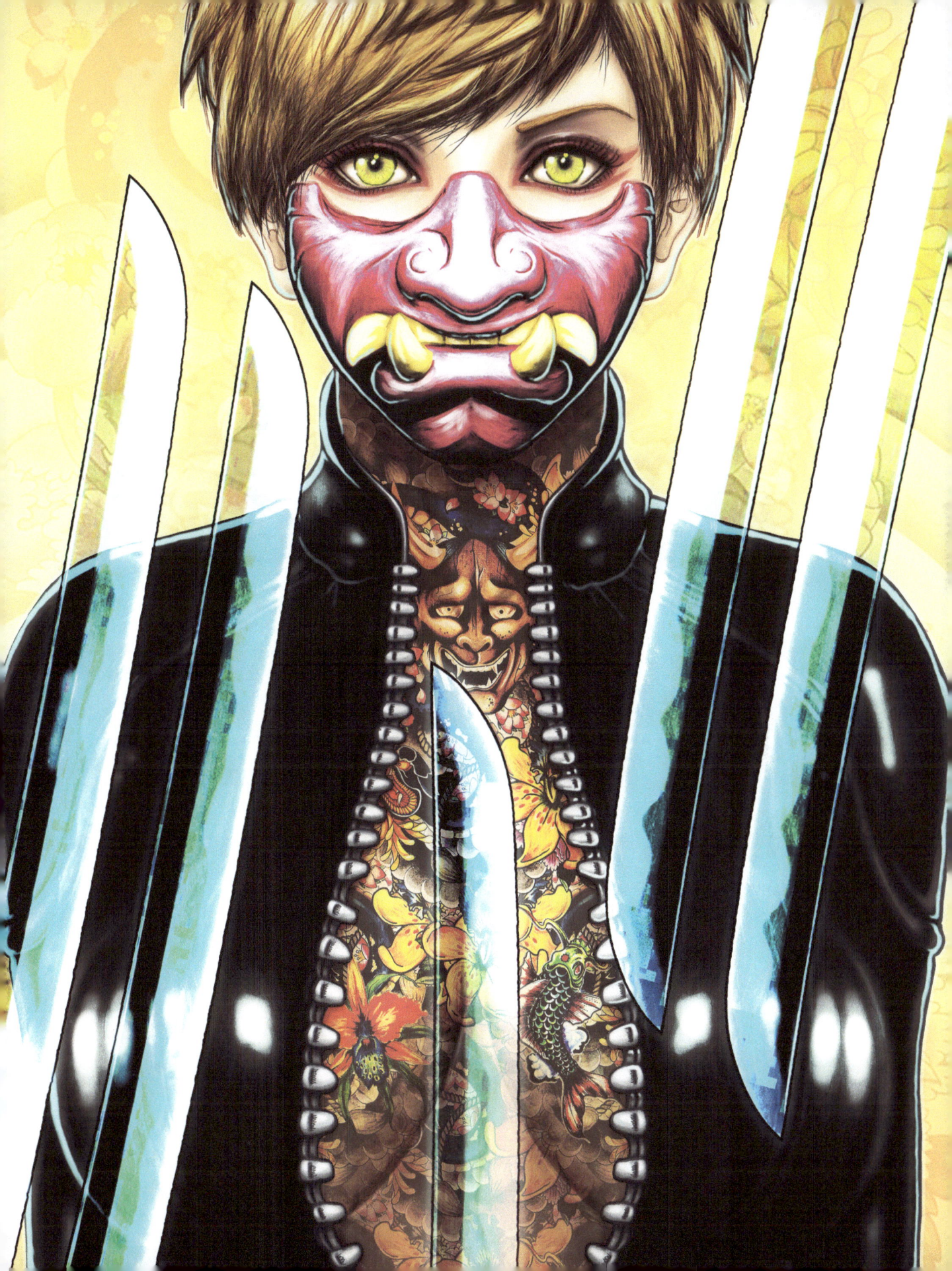

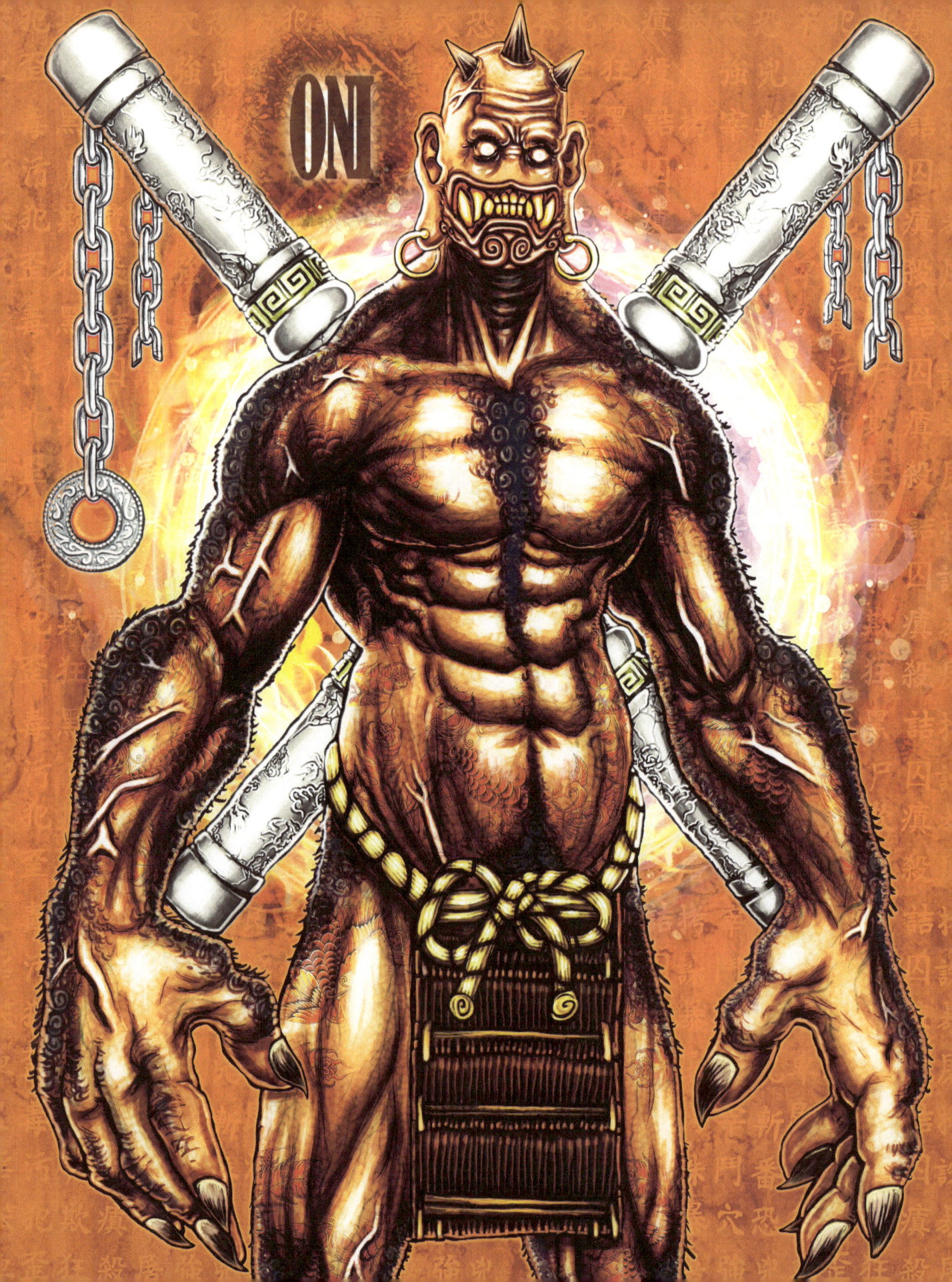

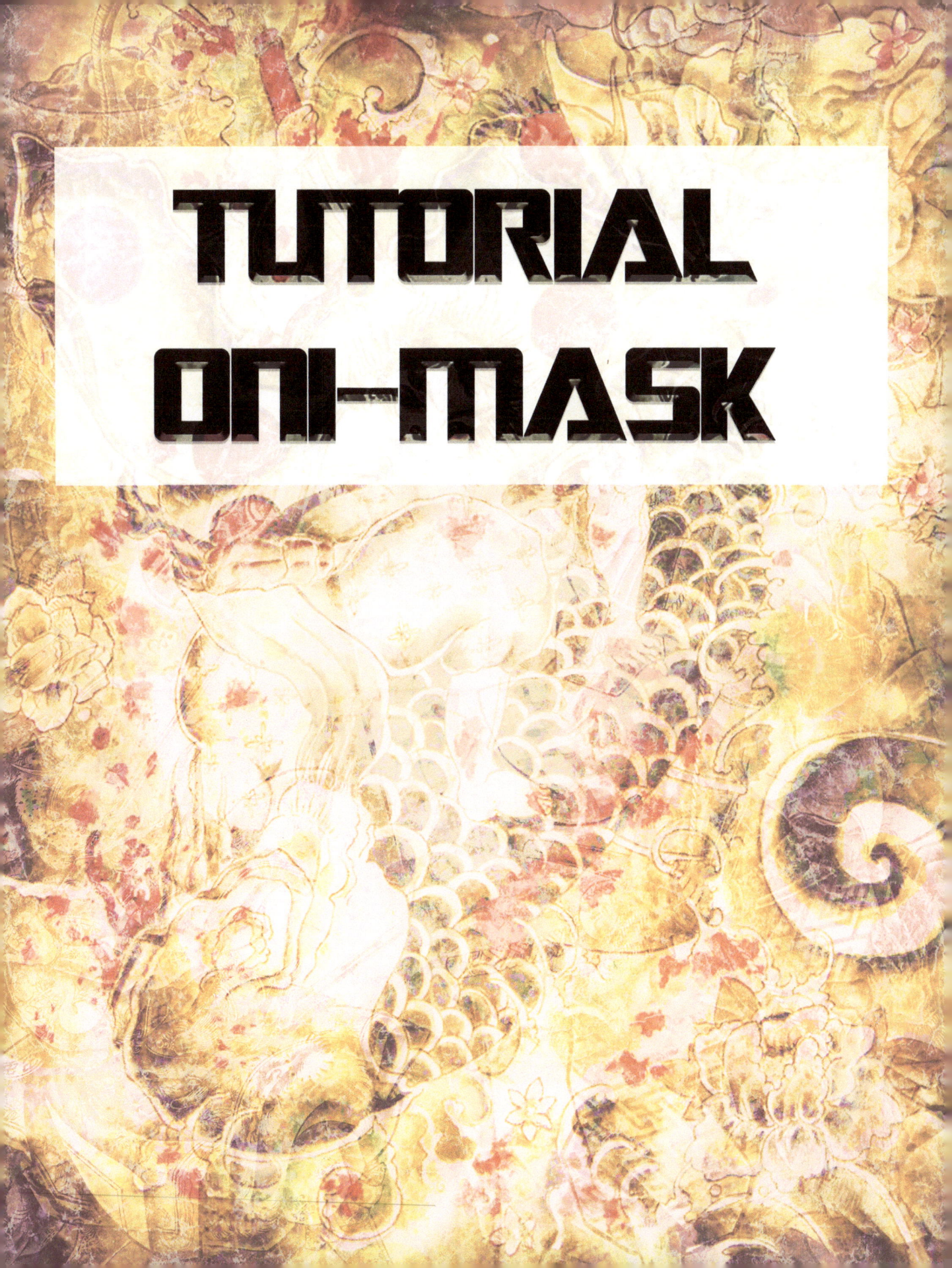

TUTORIAL
ONI-MASK

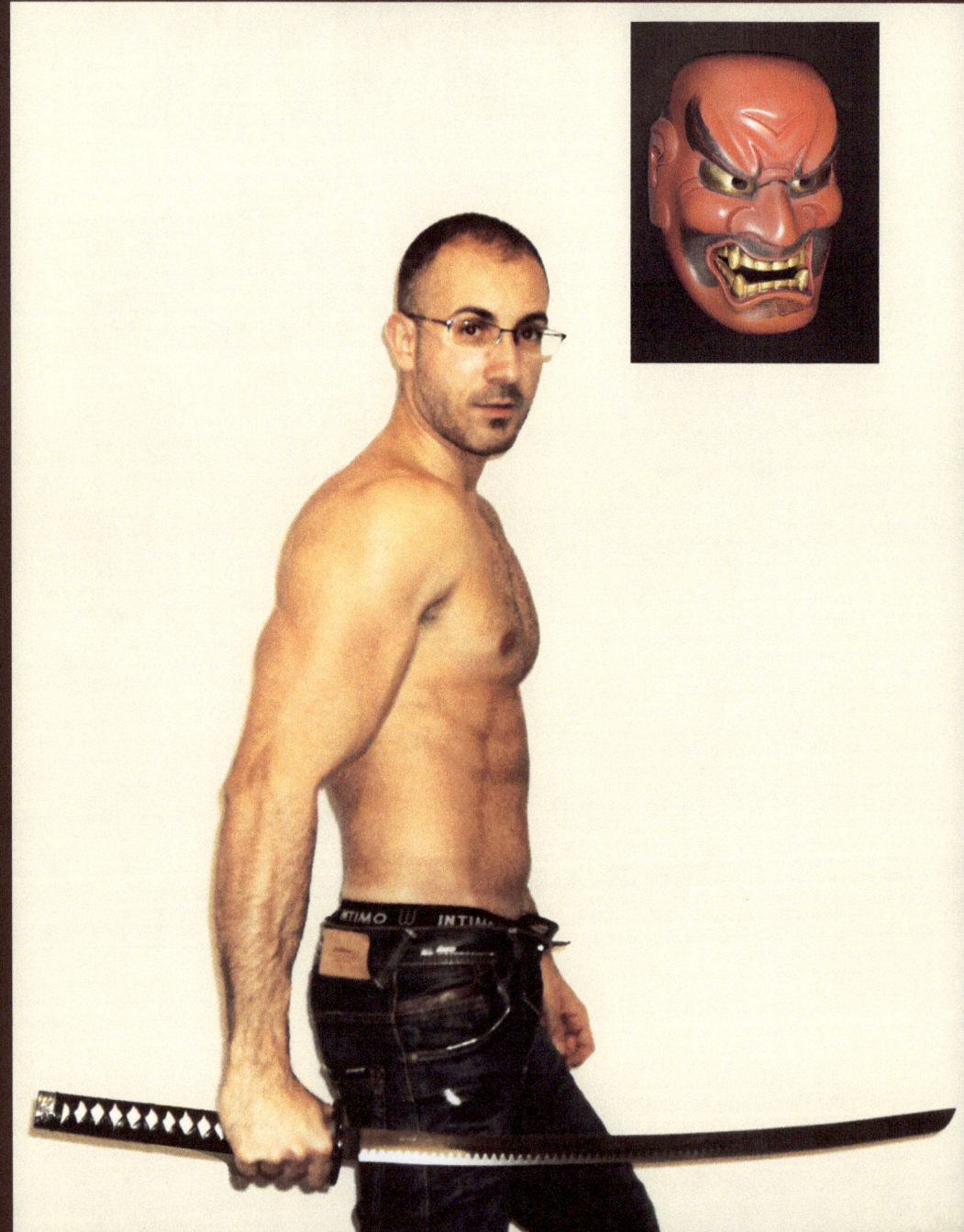

REFERENCES

ME & MASK (PHOTOS)

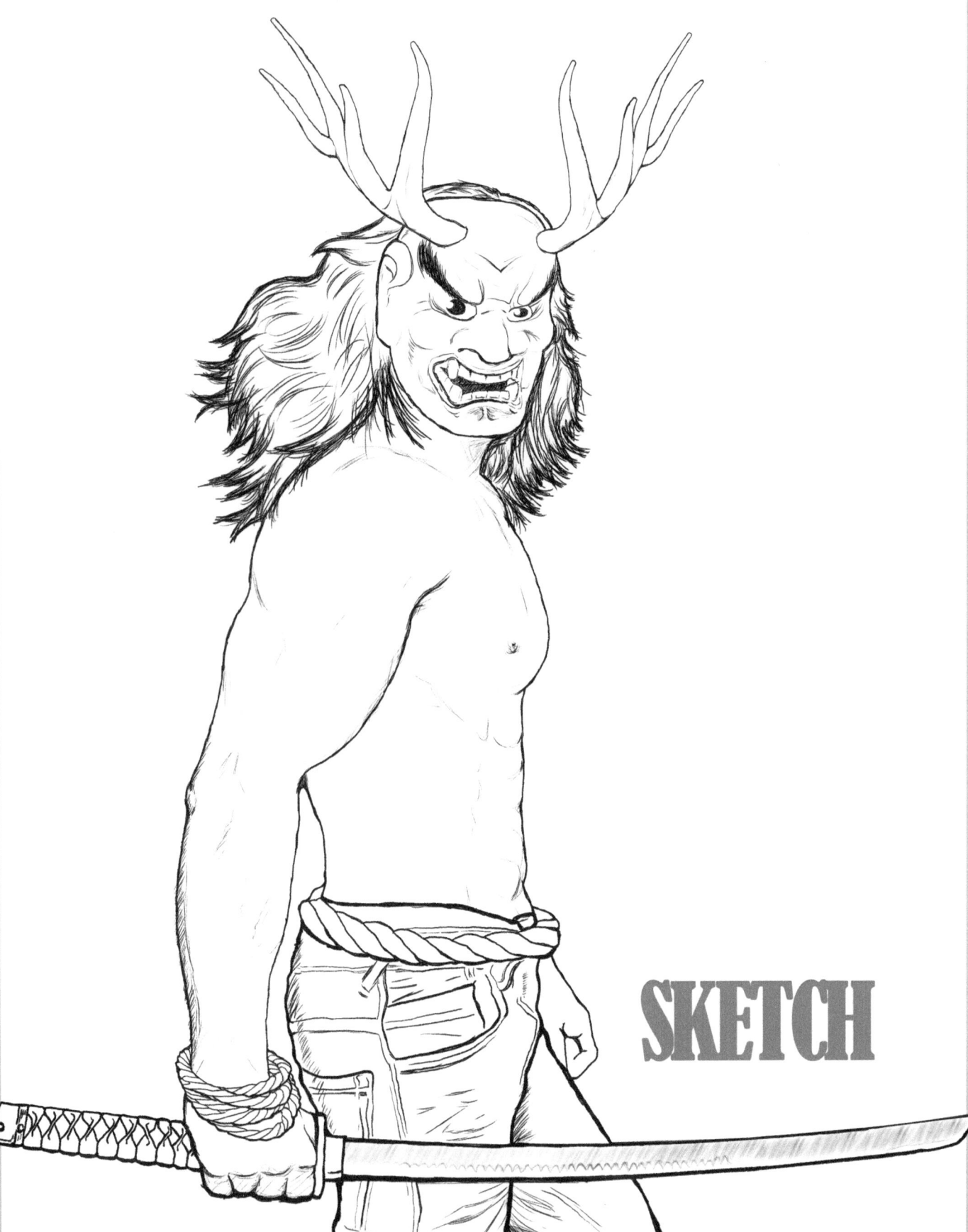

SKETCH

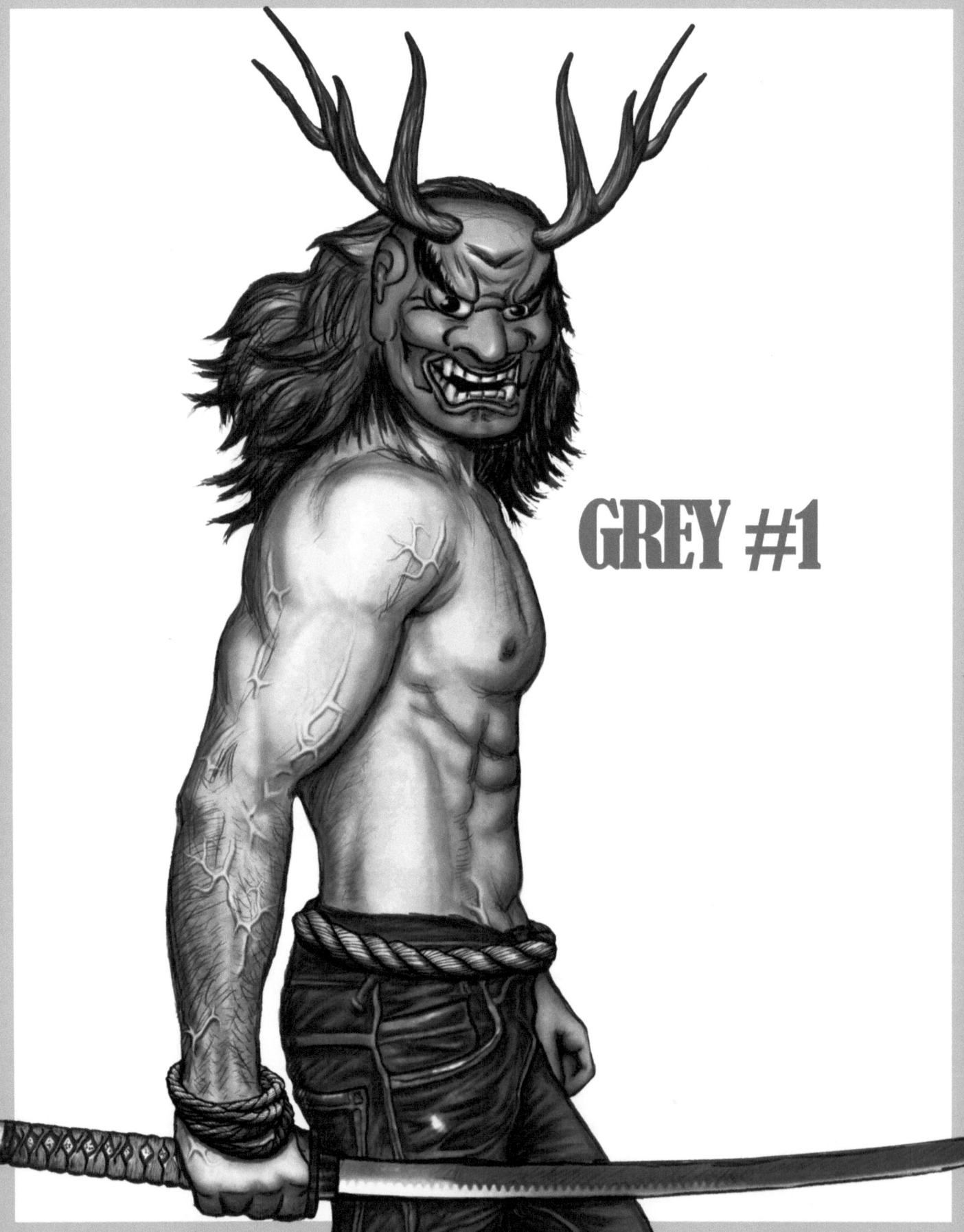

GREY #1

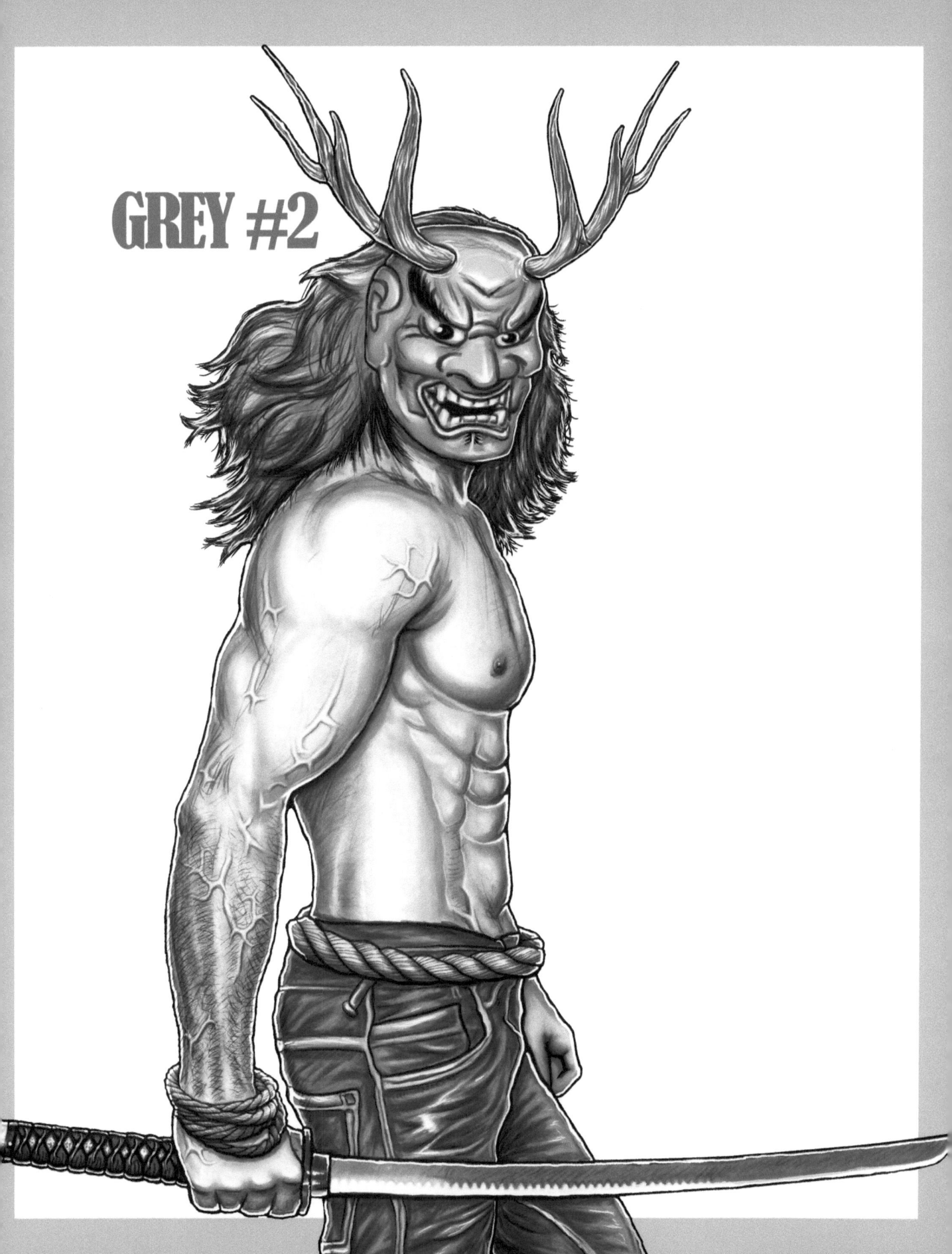

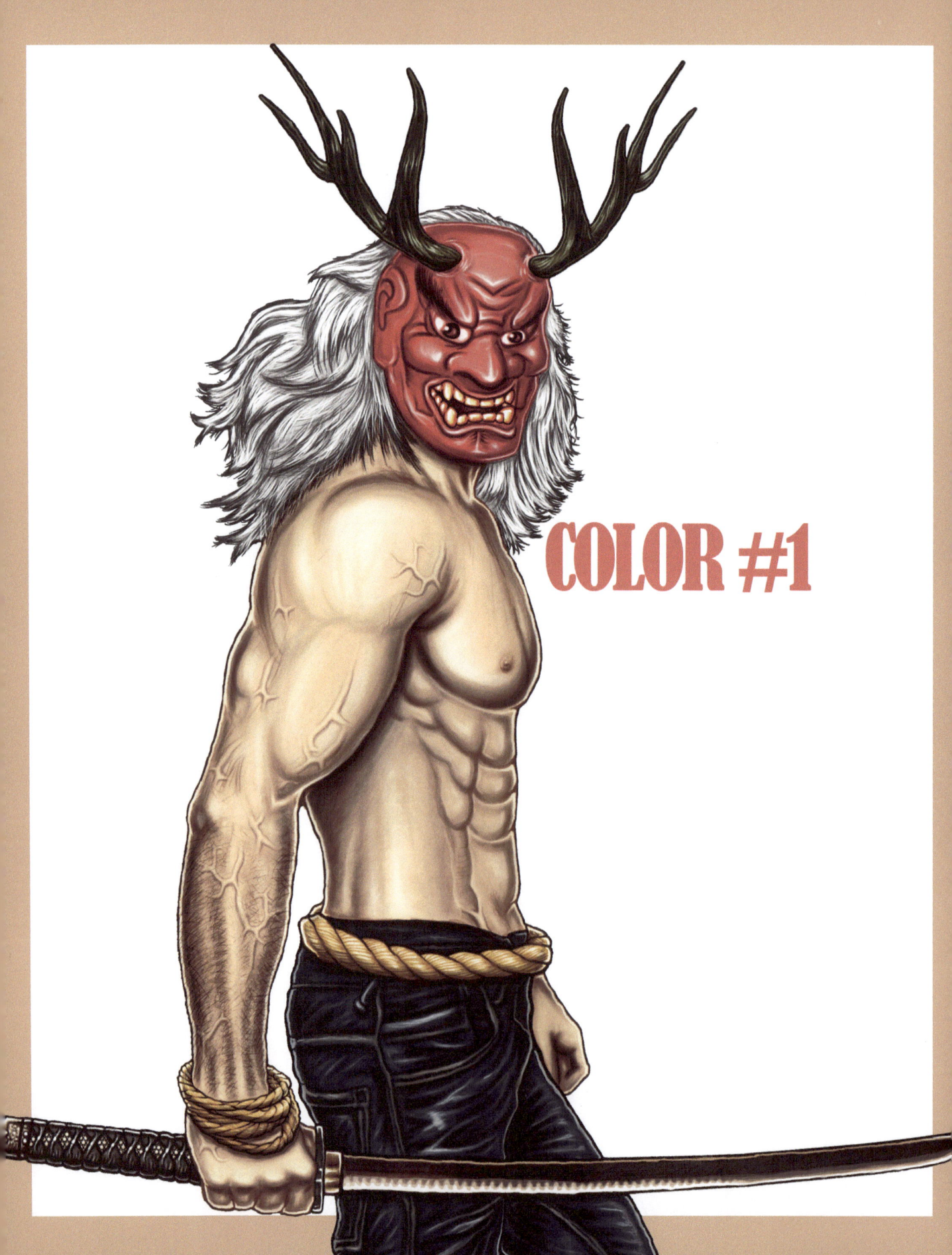

COLOR #1

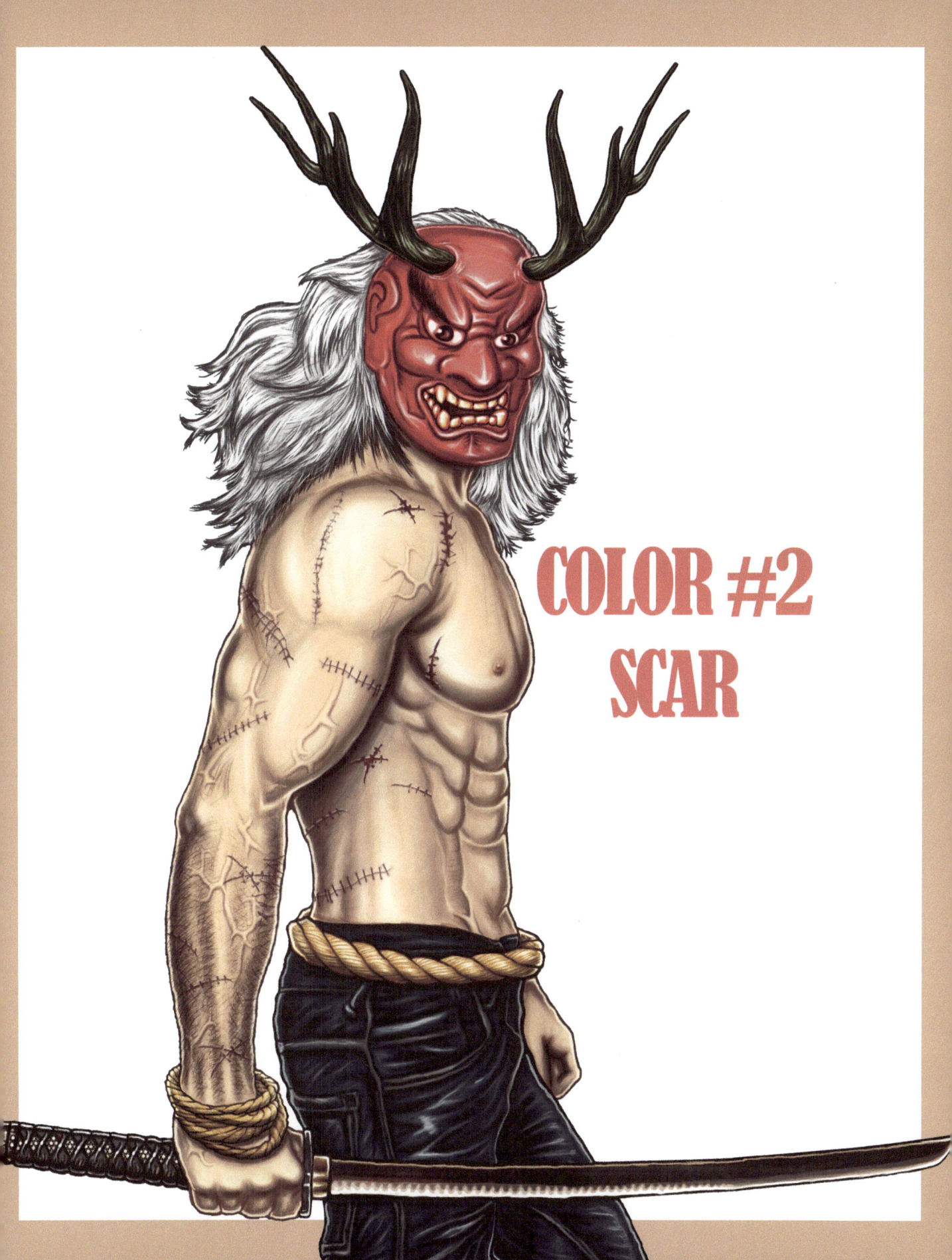

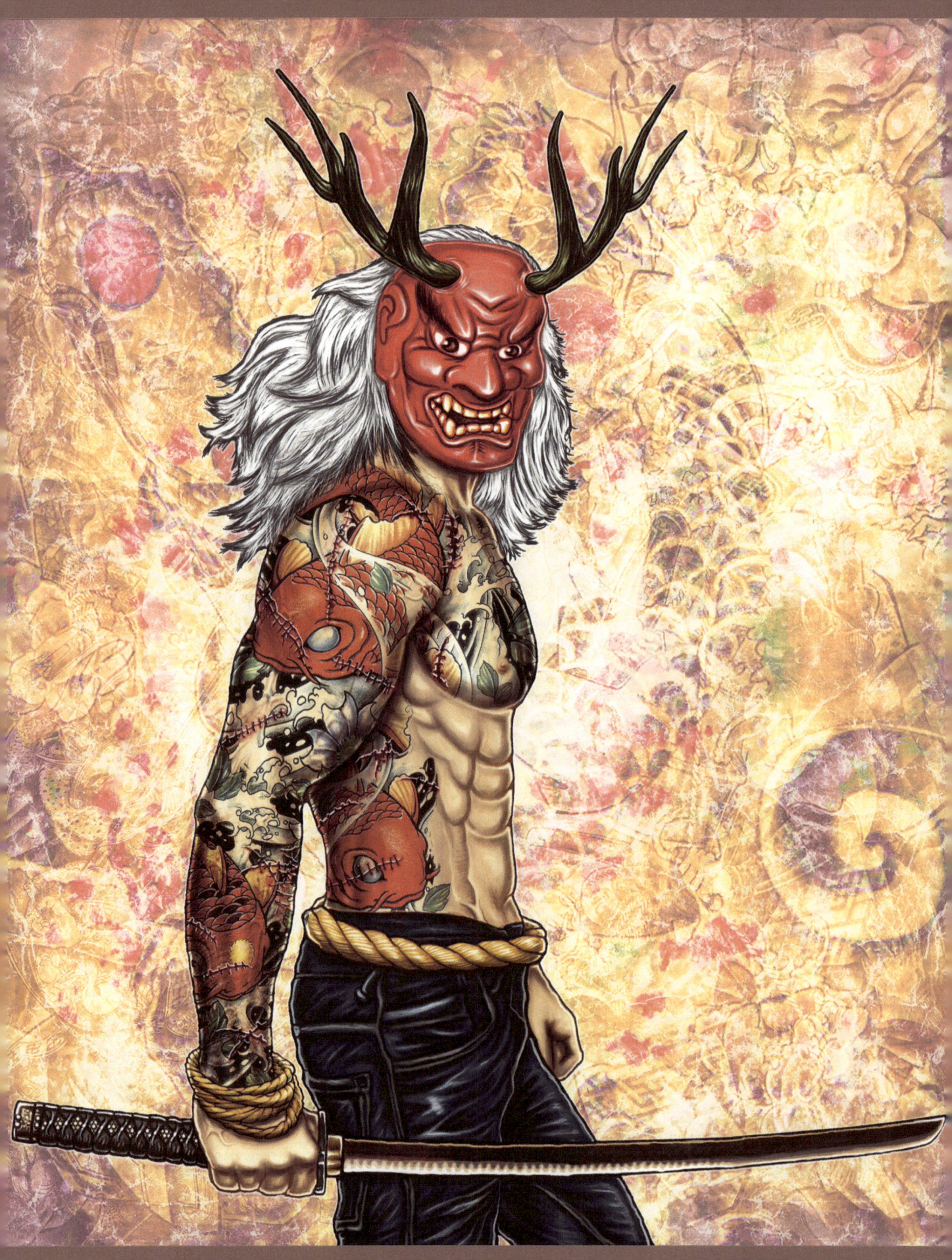

VARIOUS

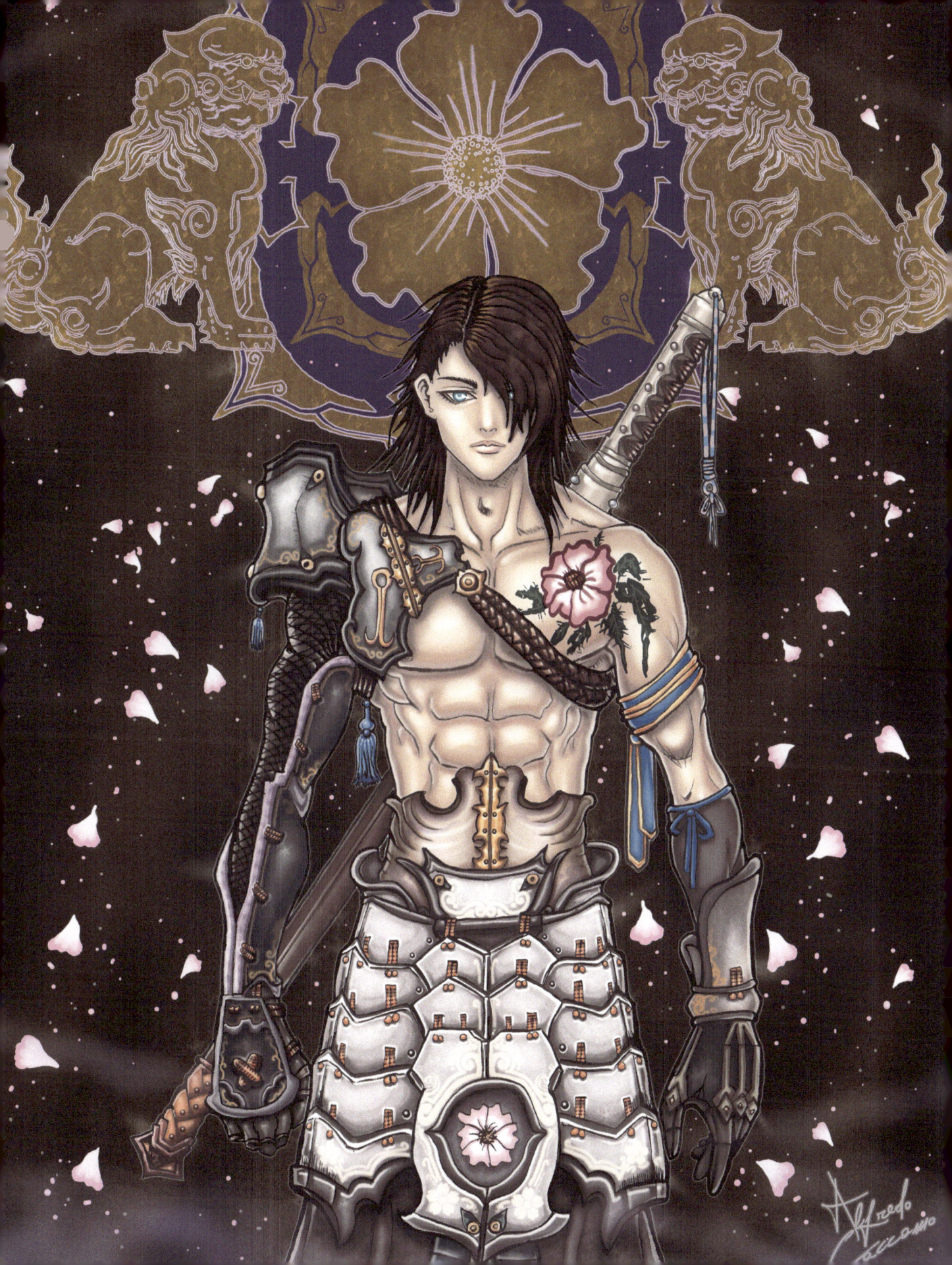

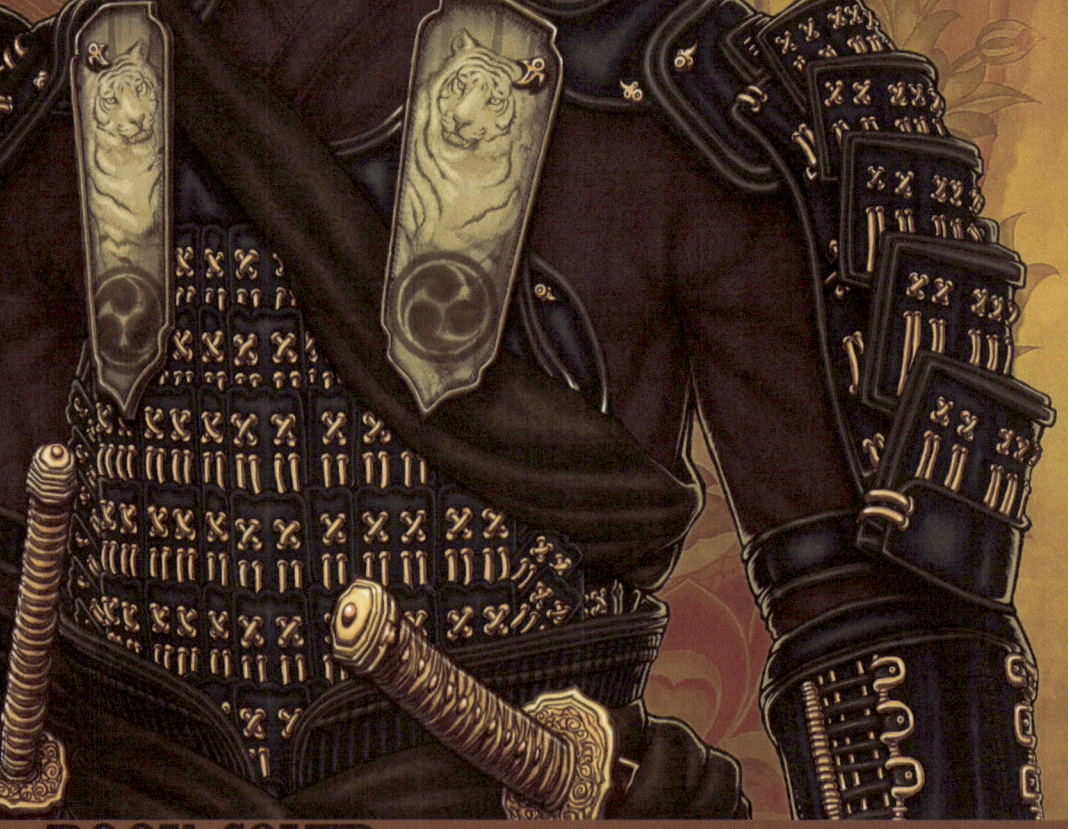

SECRET NINJA SCROLLS

BOOK 1

ALFREDO CACCAMO

a-BOOK

BOOK COVER

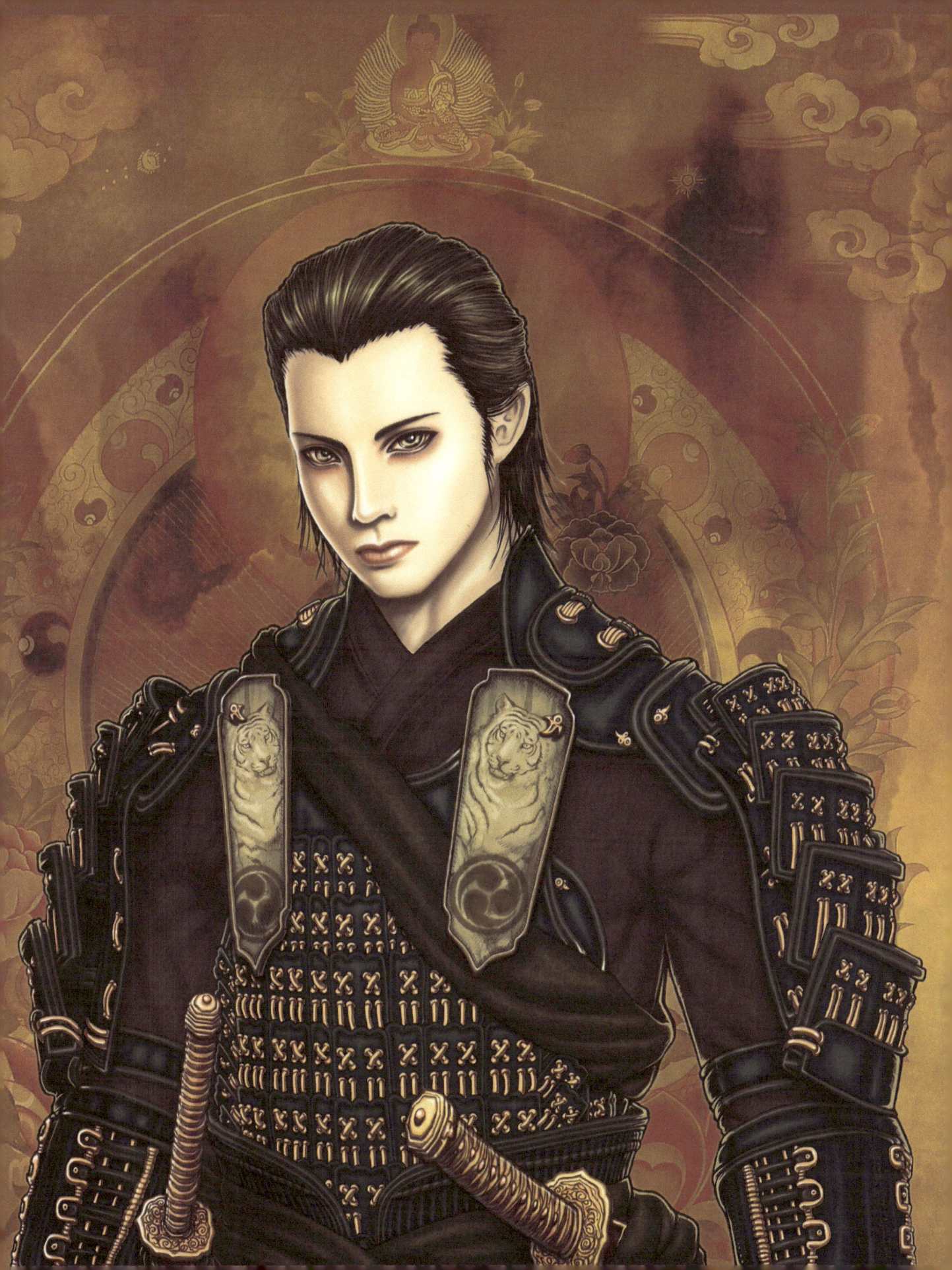

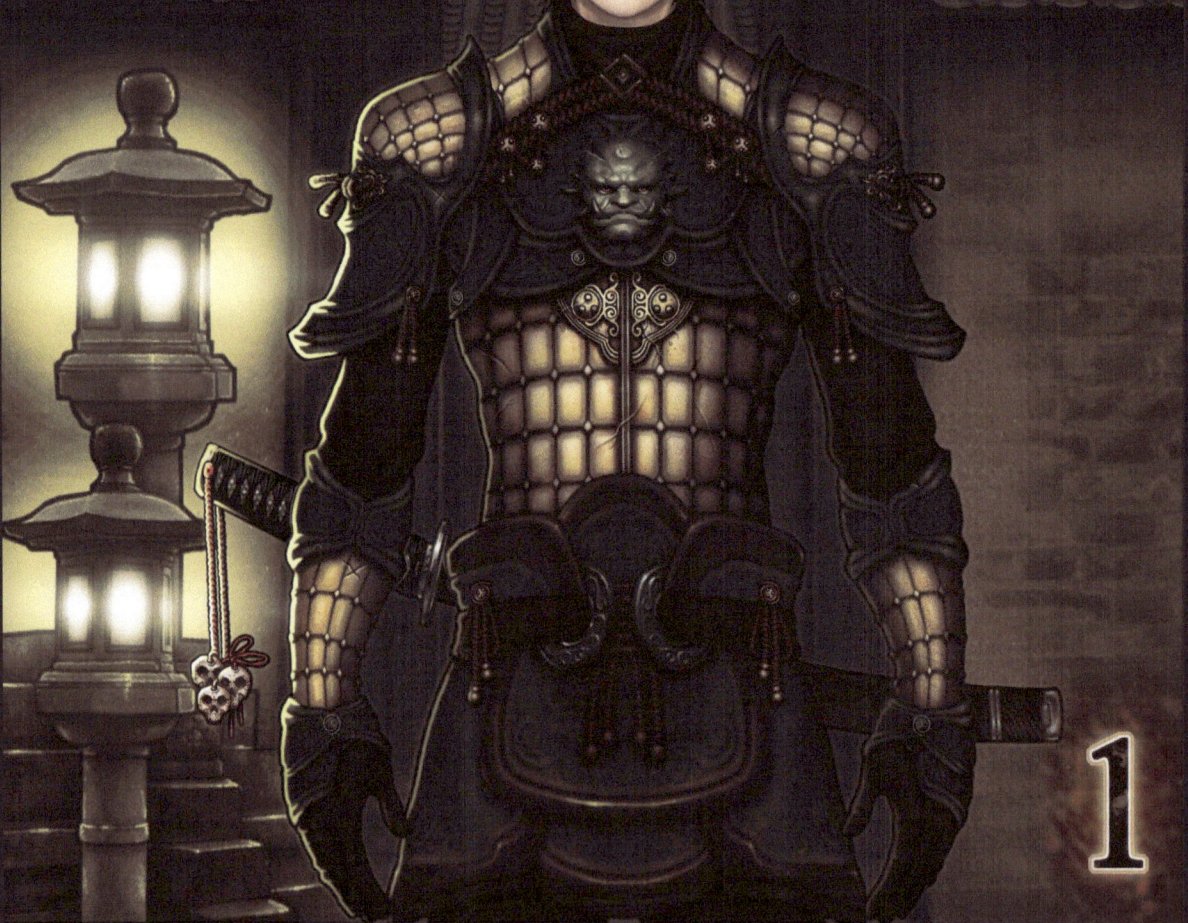

I ROTOLI SEGRETI DEI NINJA

ALFREDO CACCAMO

1

BOOK COVER

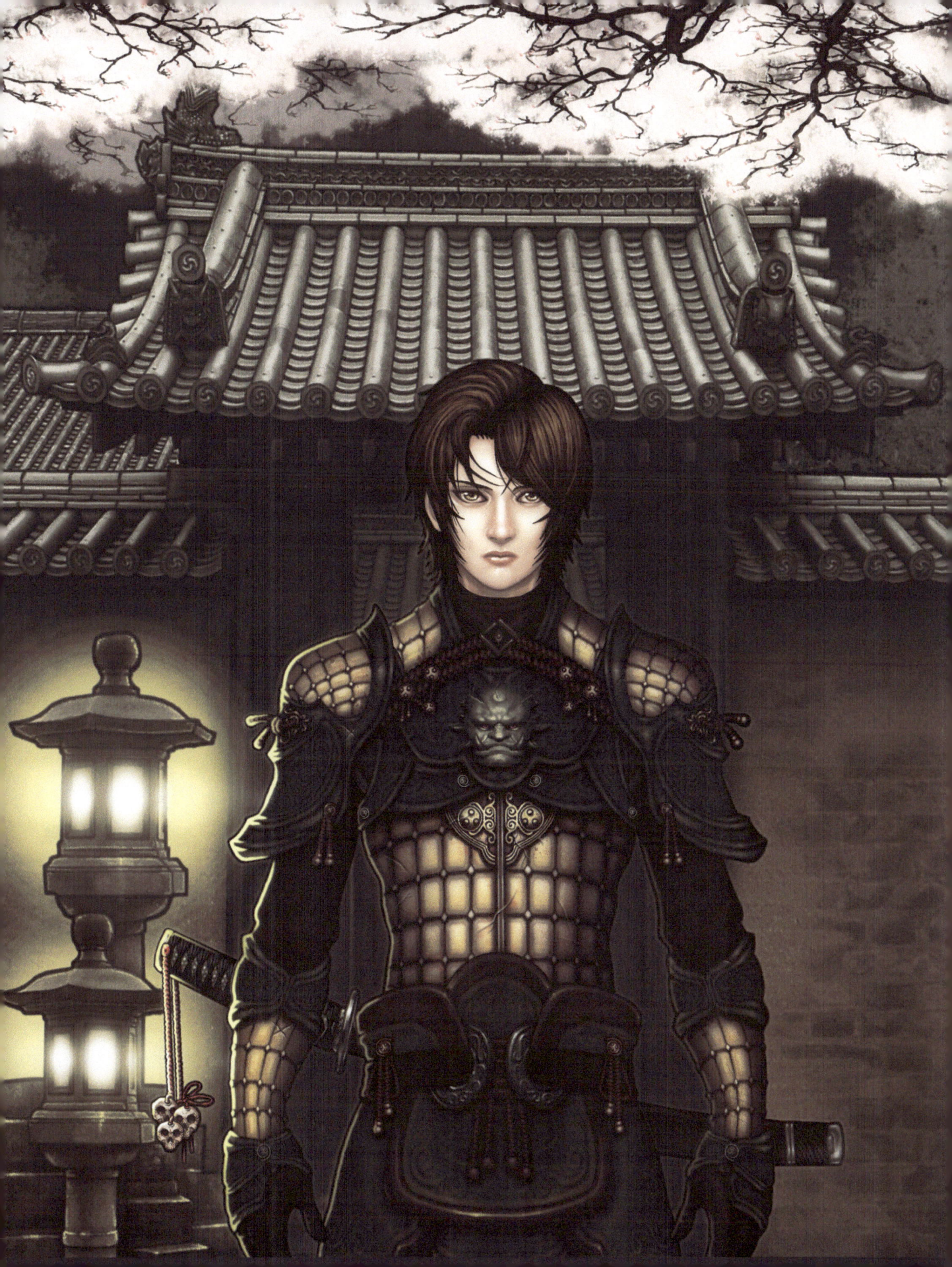

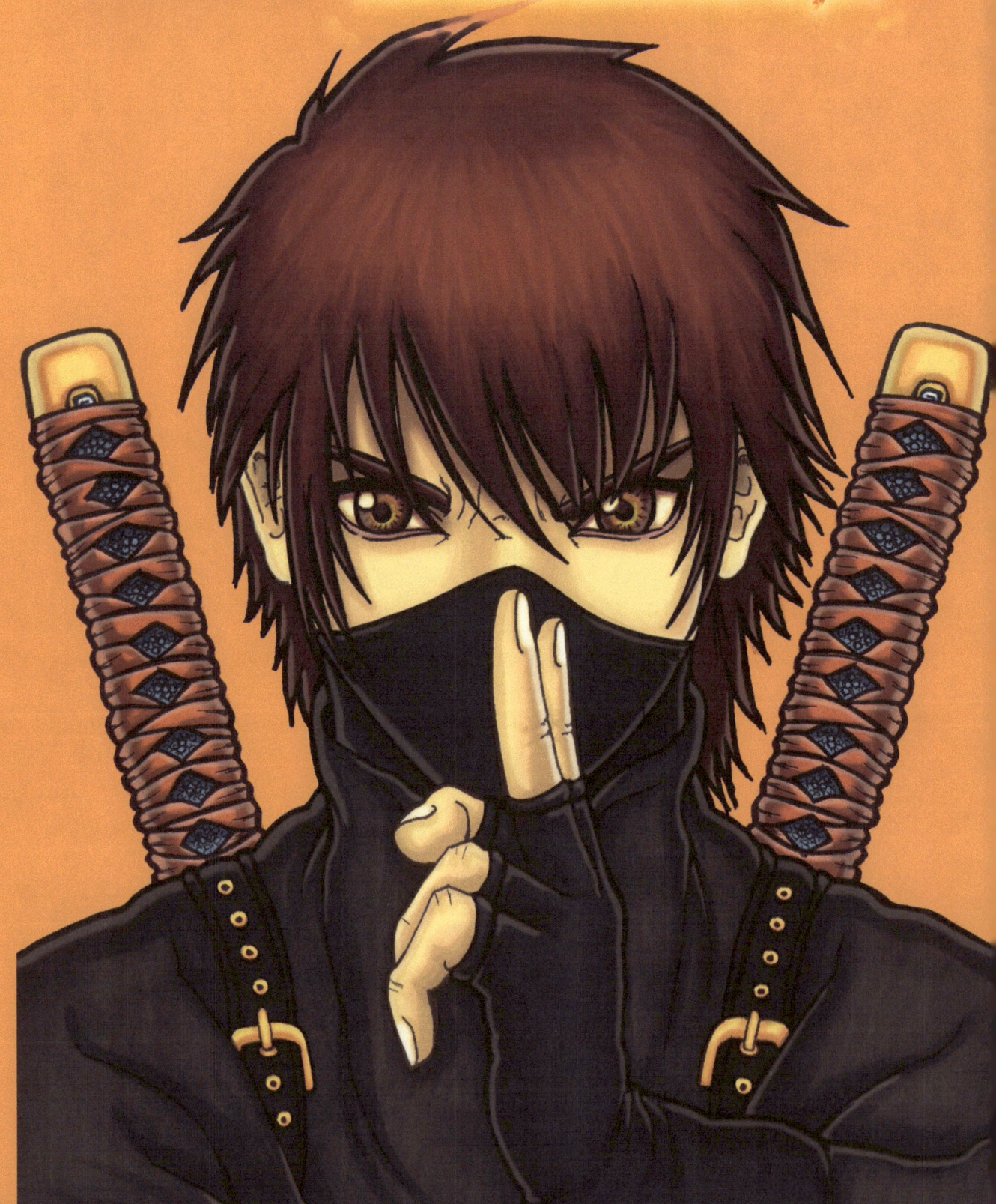

BOOK COVER : I ROTOLI SEGRETI DEI NINJA 1

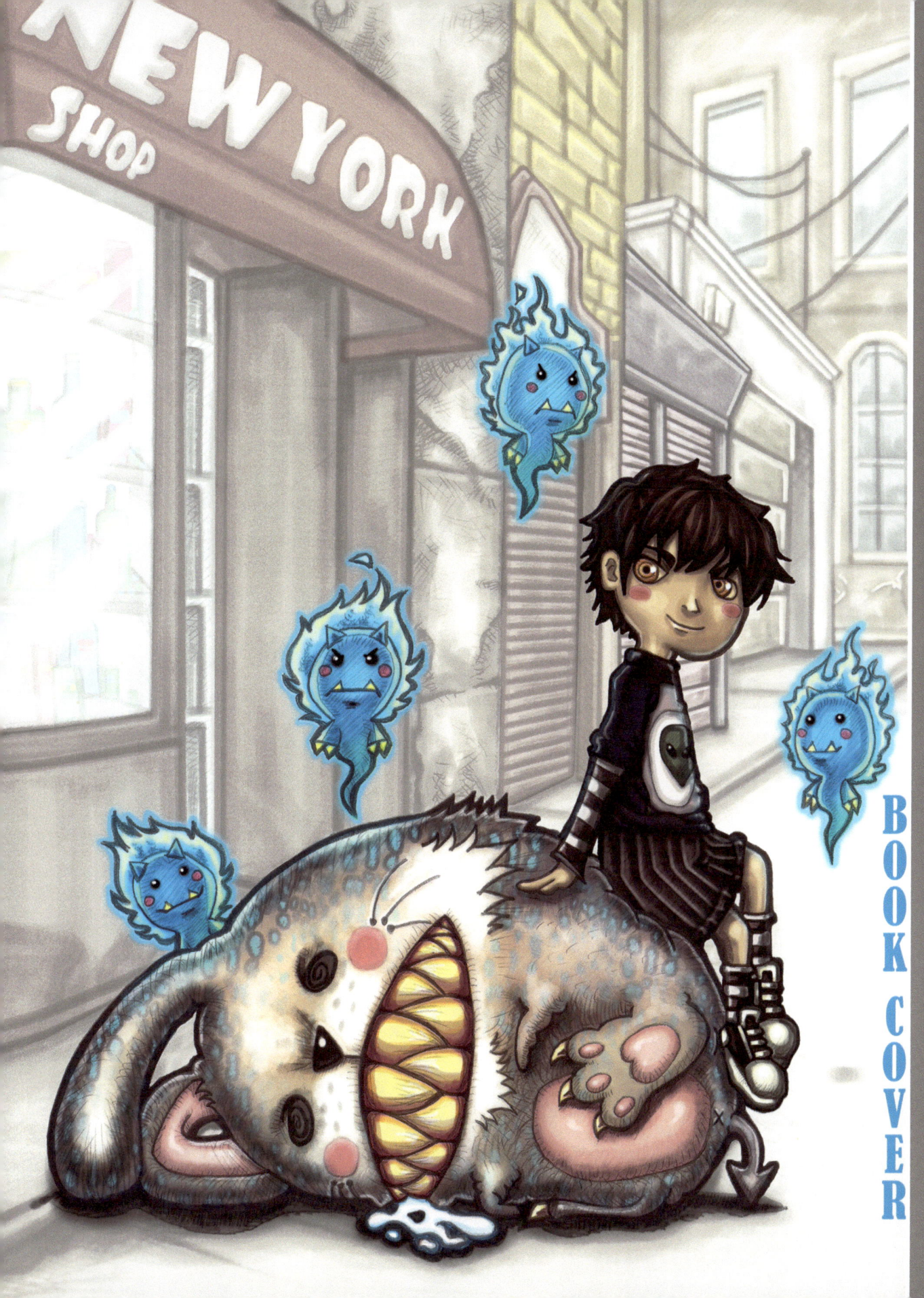

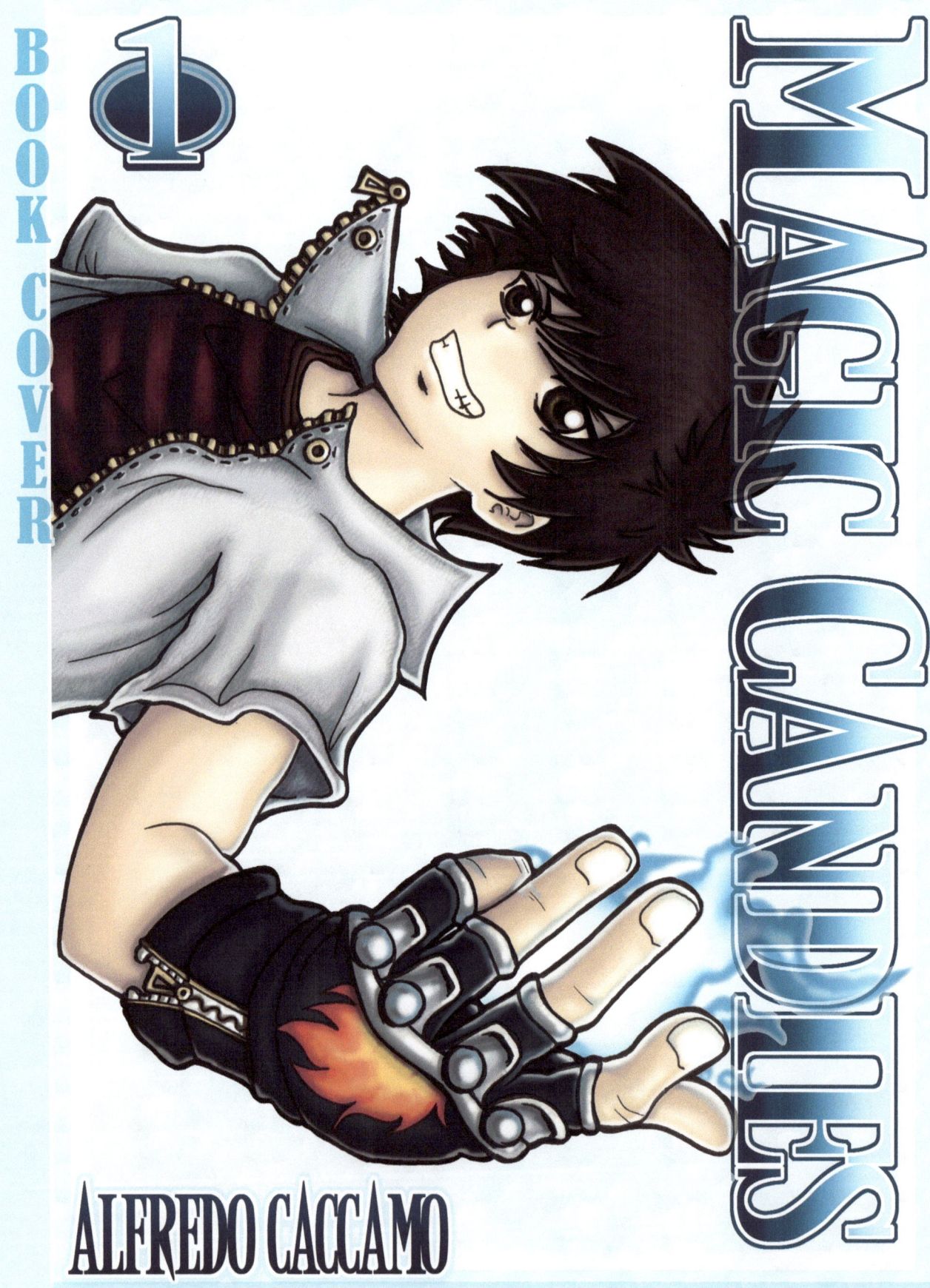

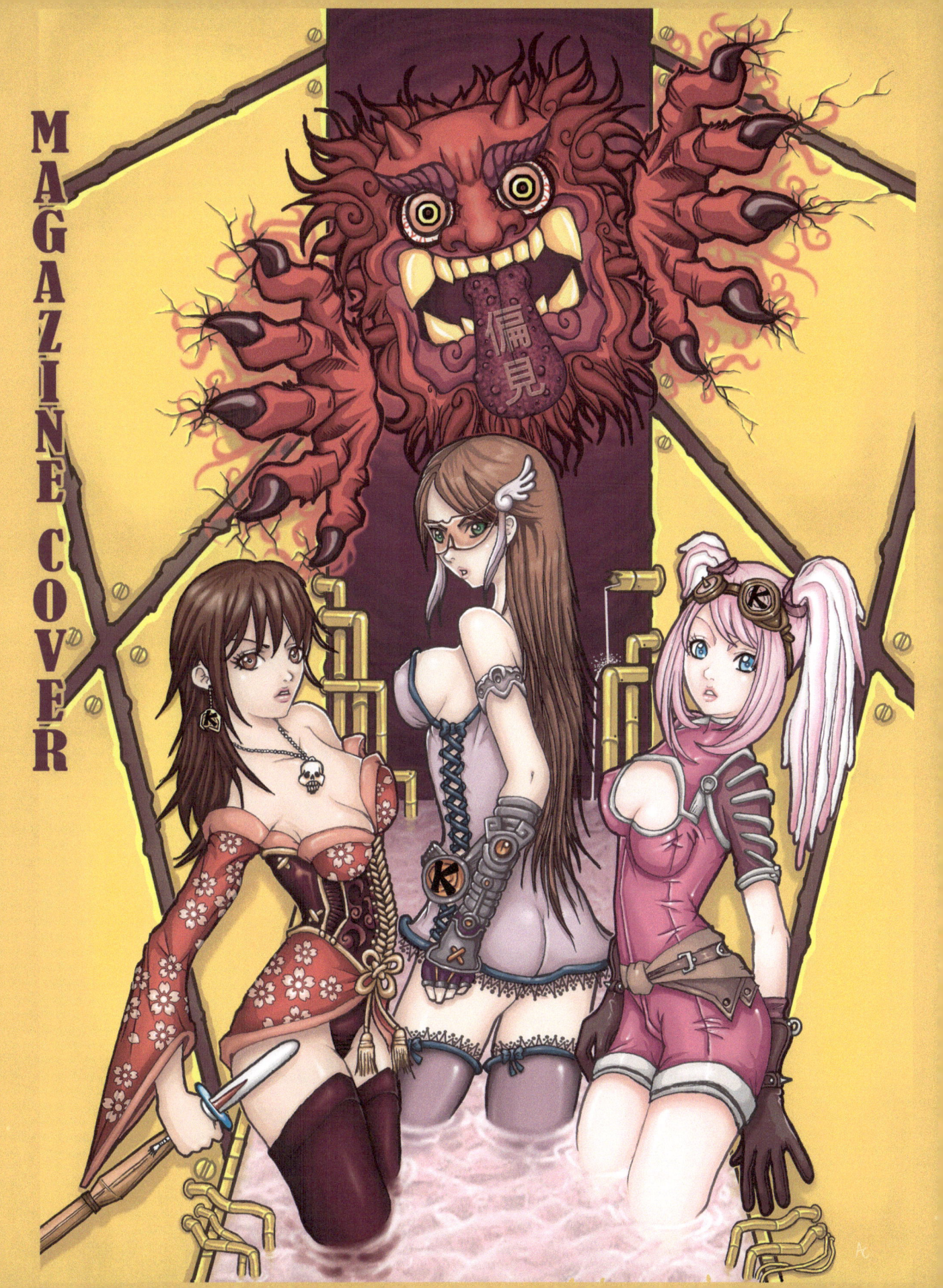

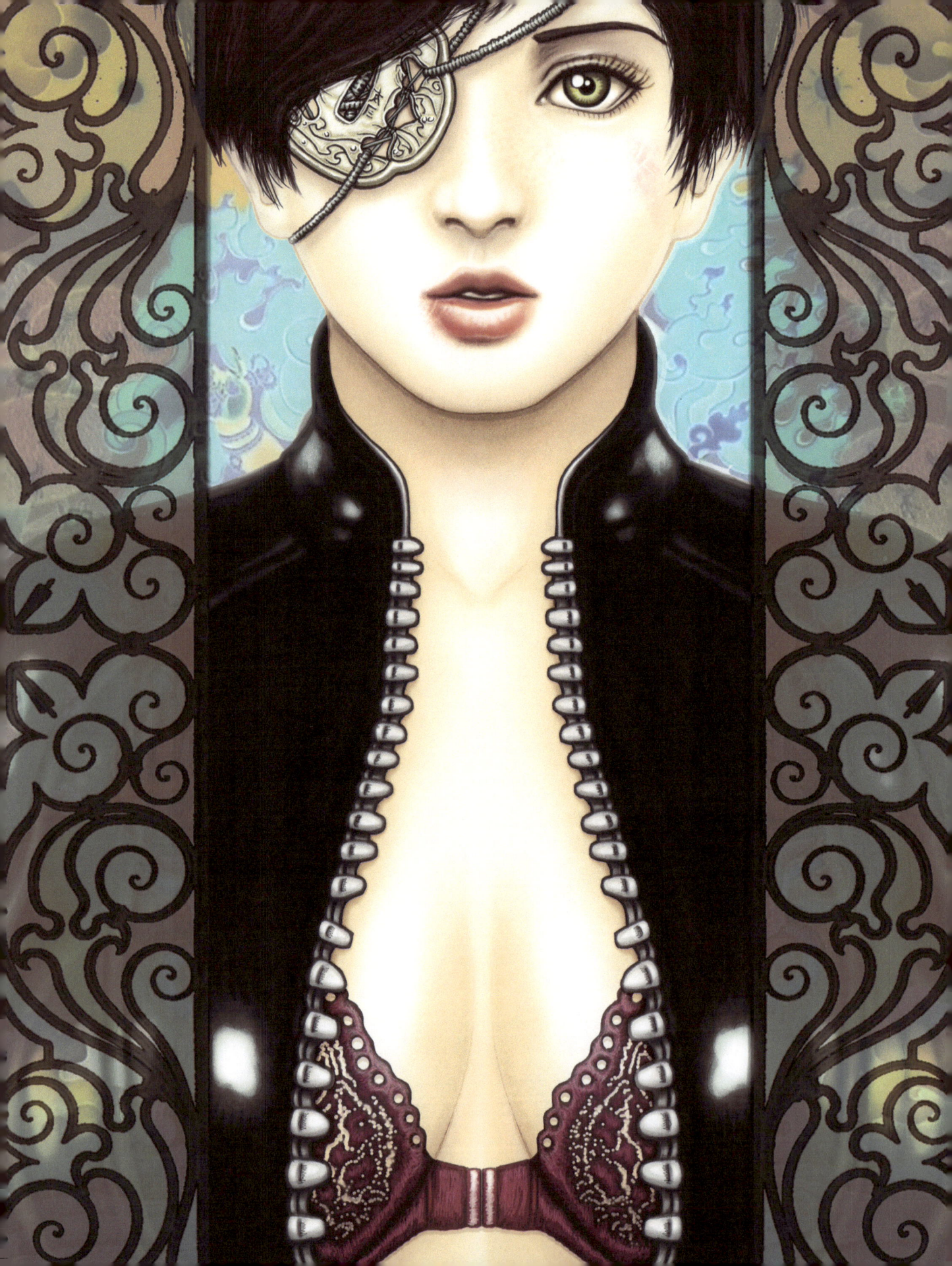

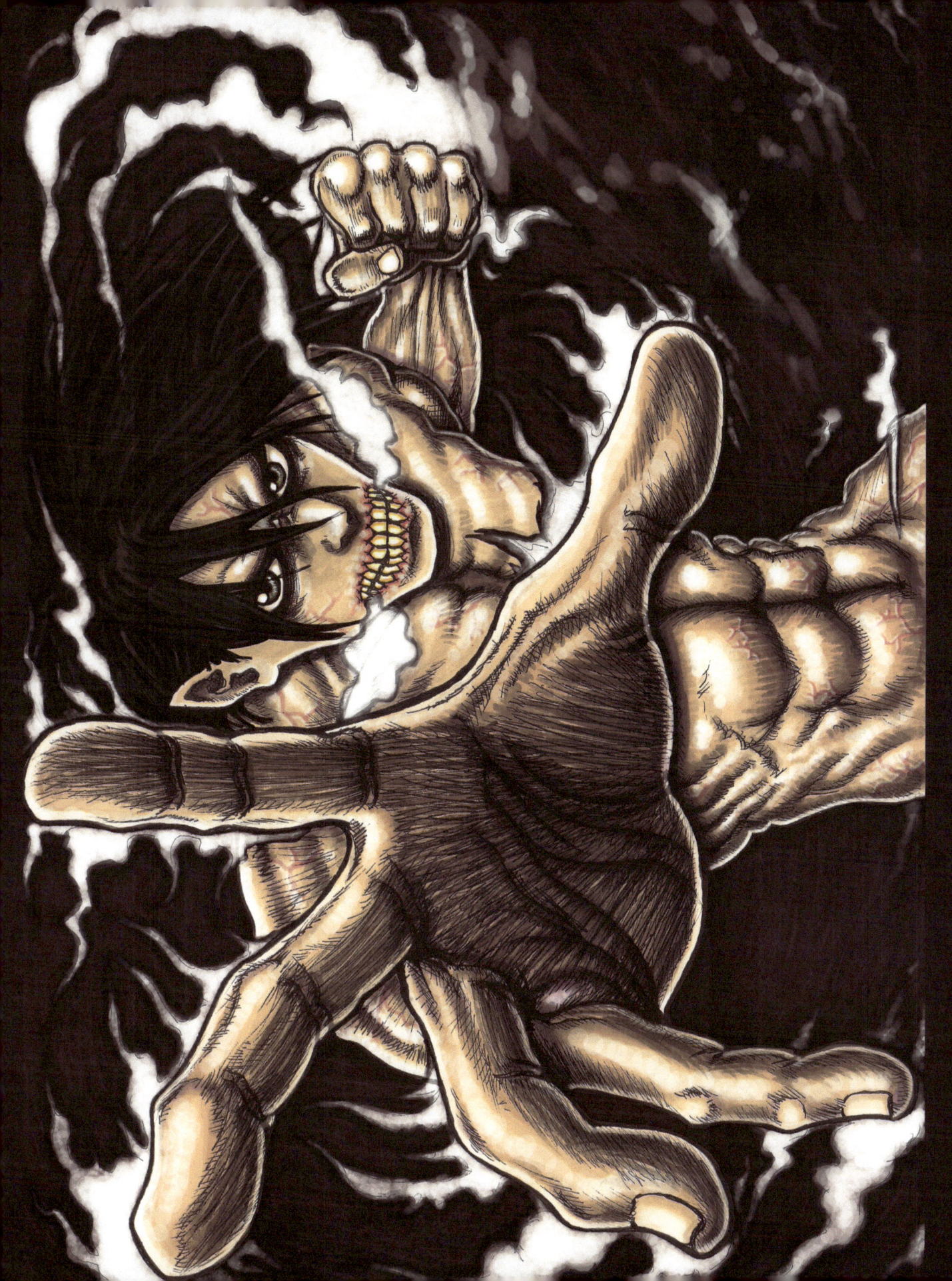

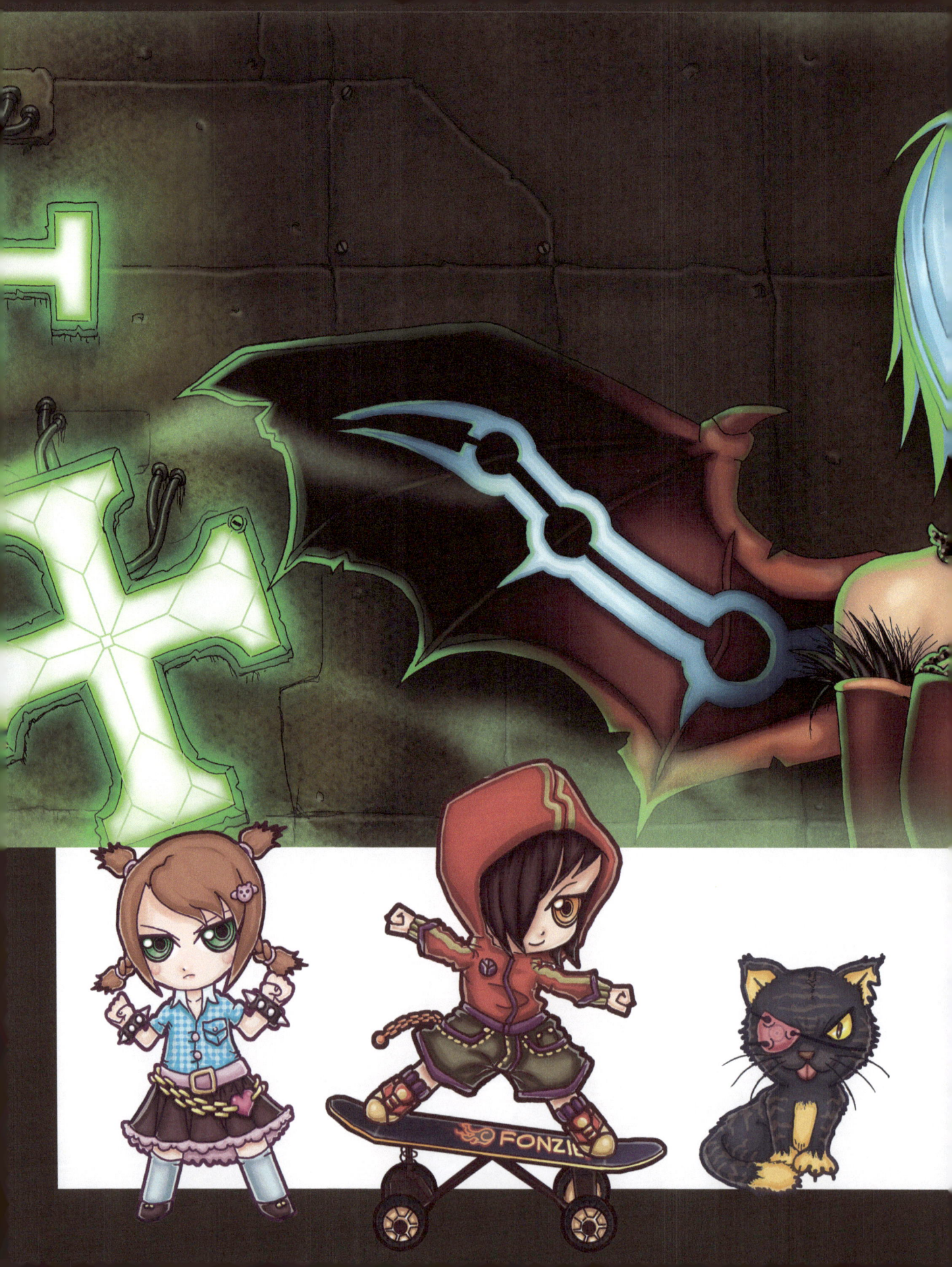

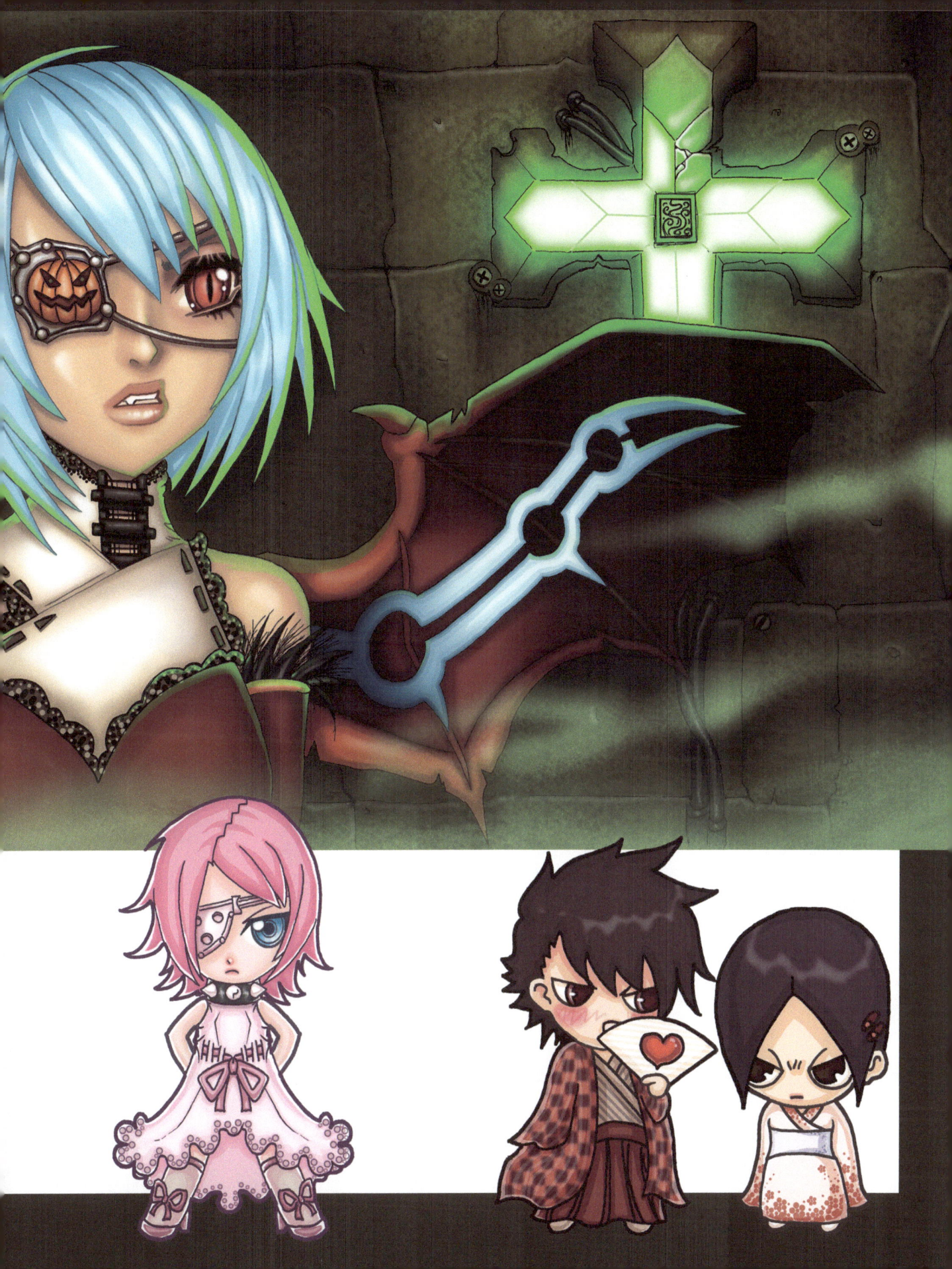

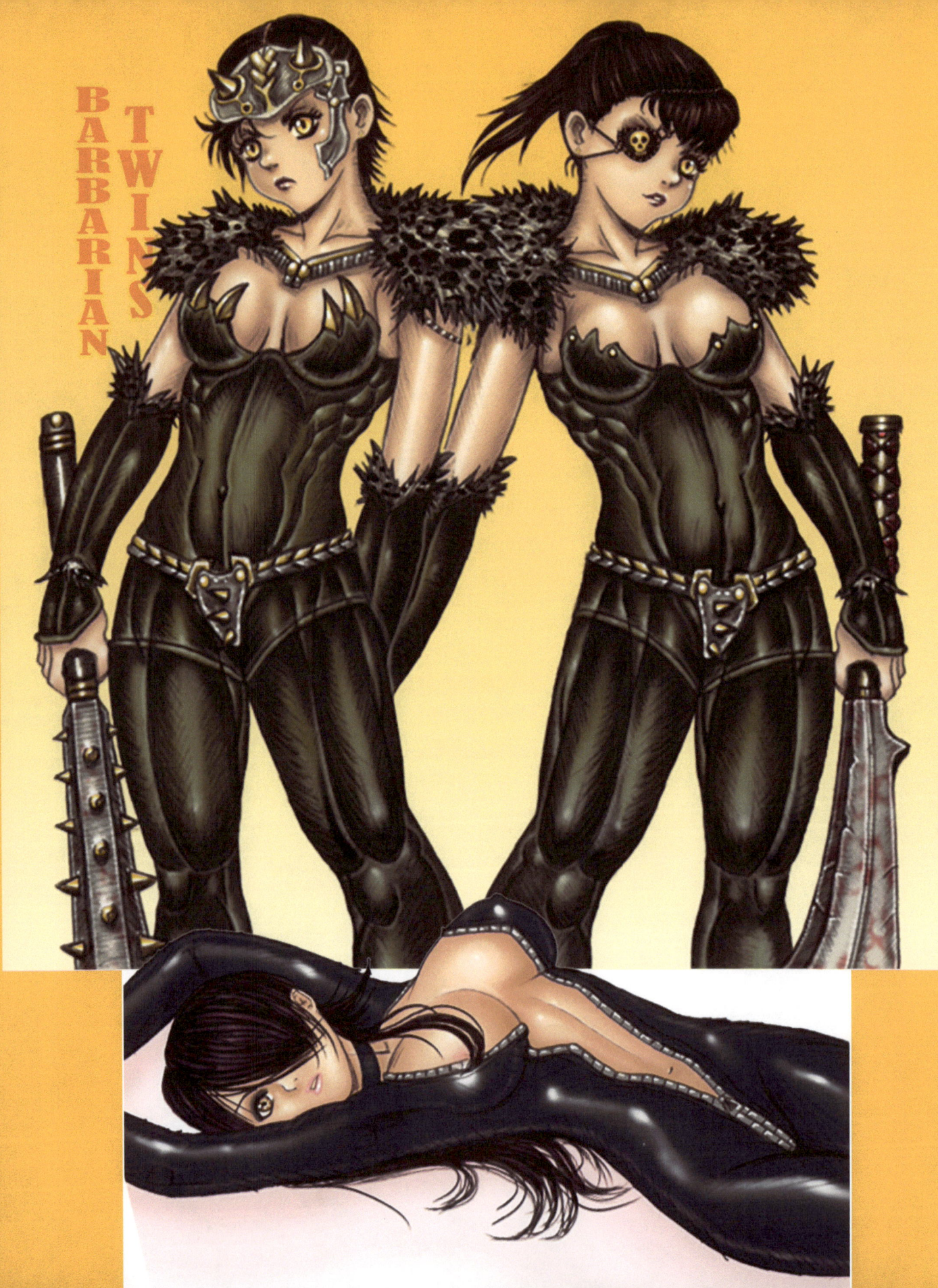

BARBARIAN TWINS

BLACK NINJAS

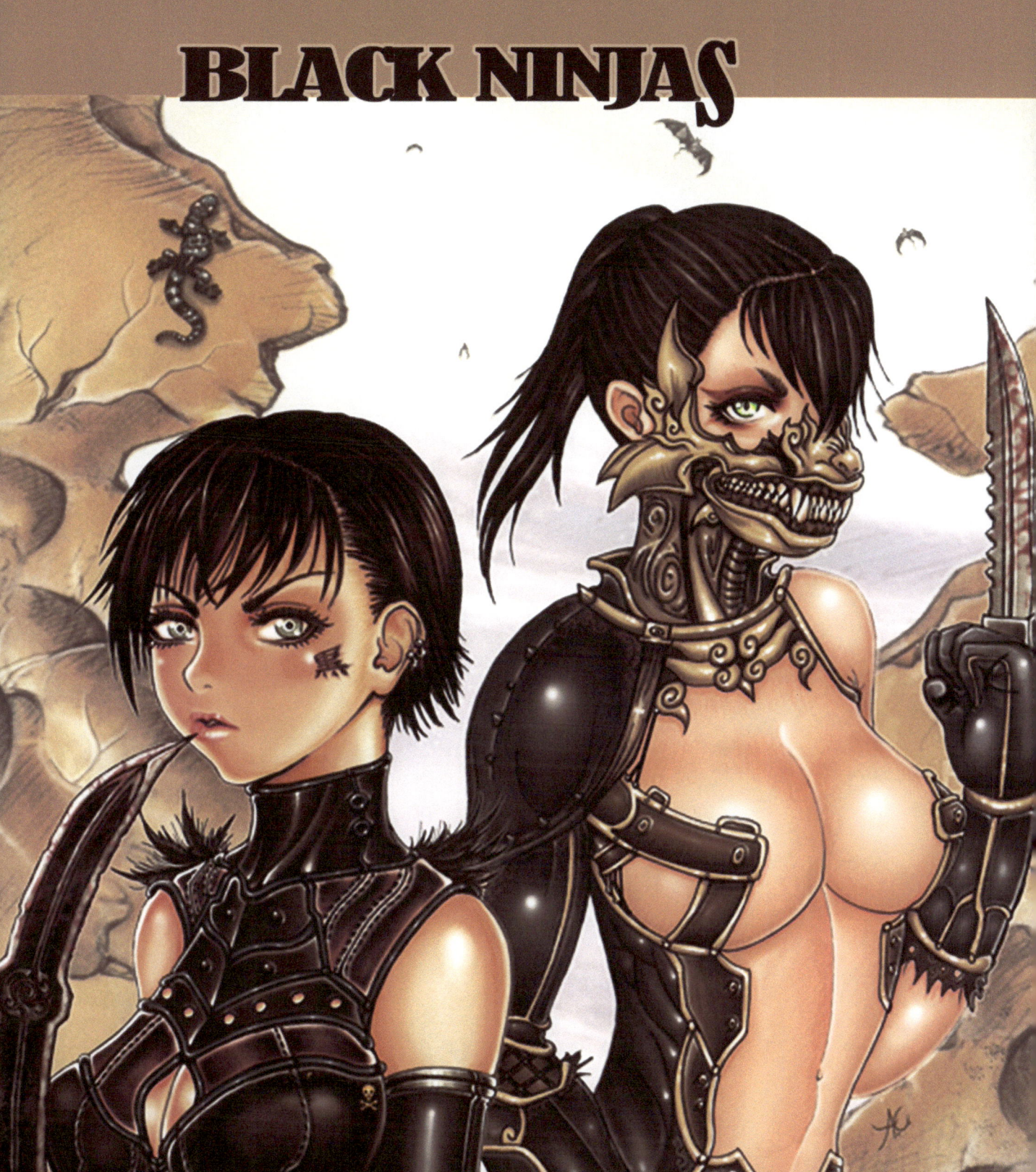

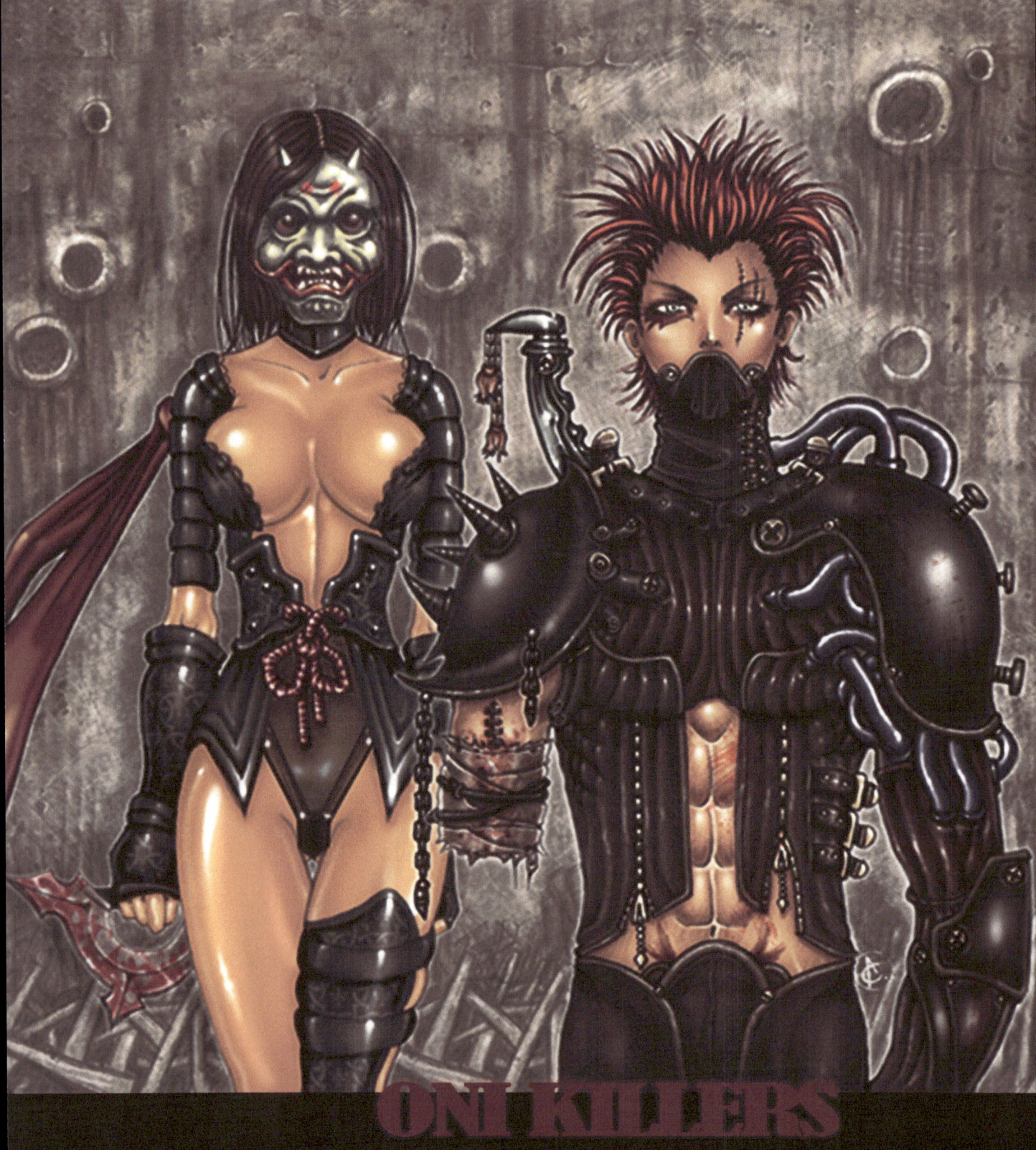

ONI KILLERS

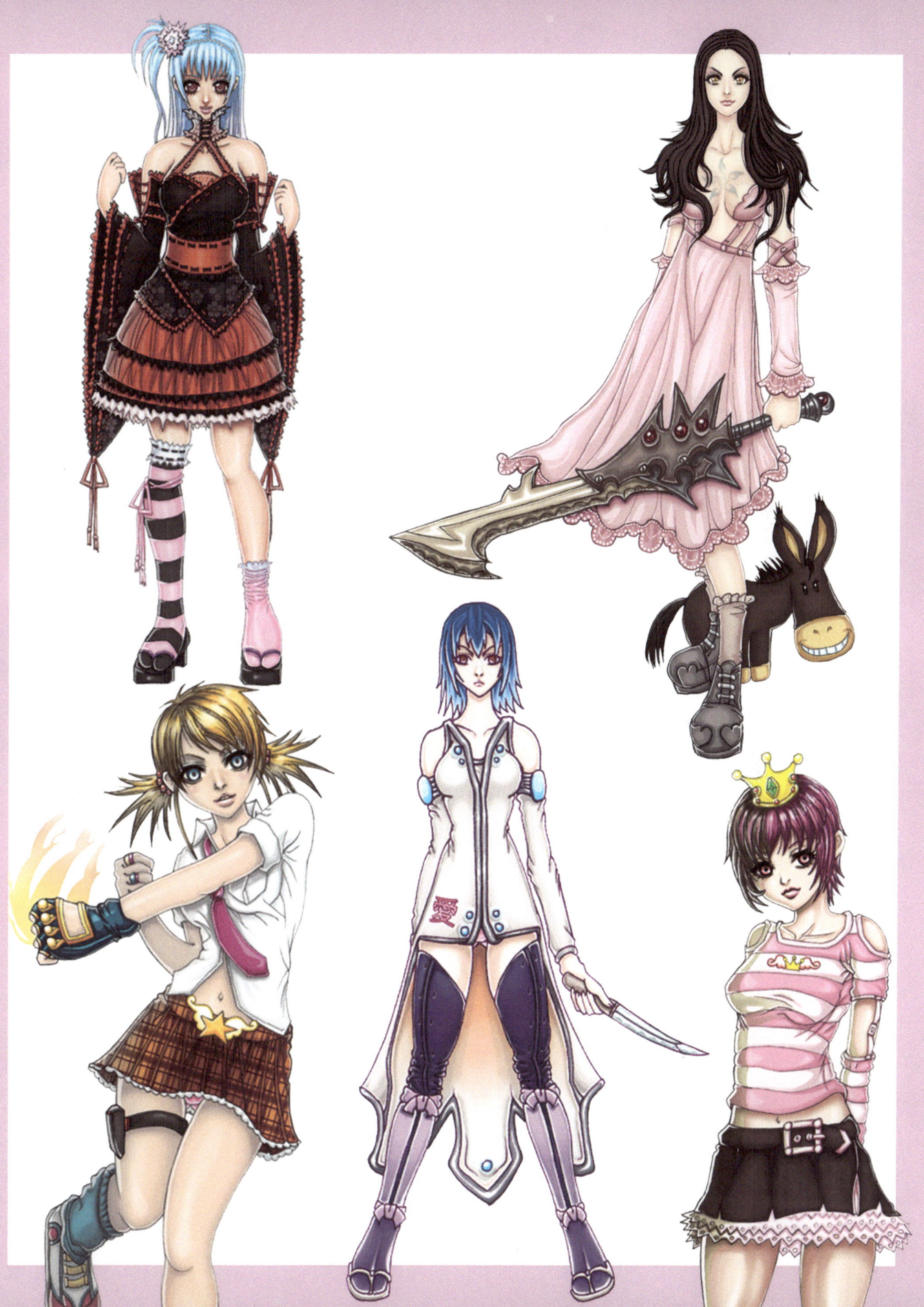

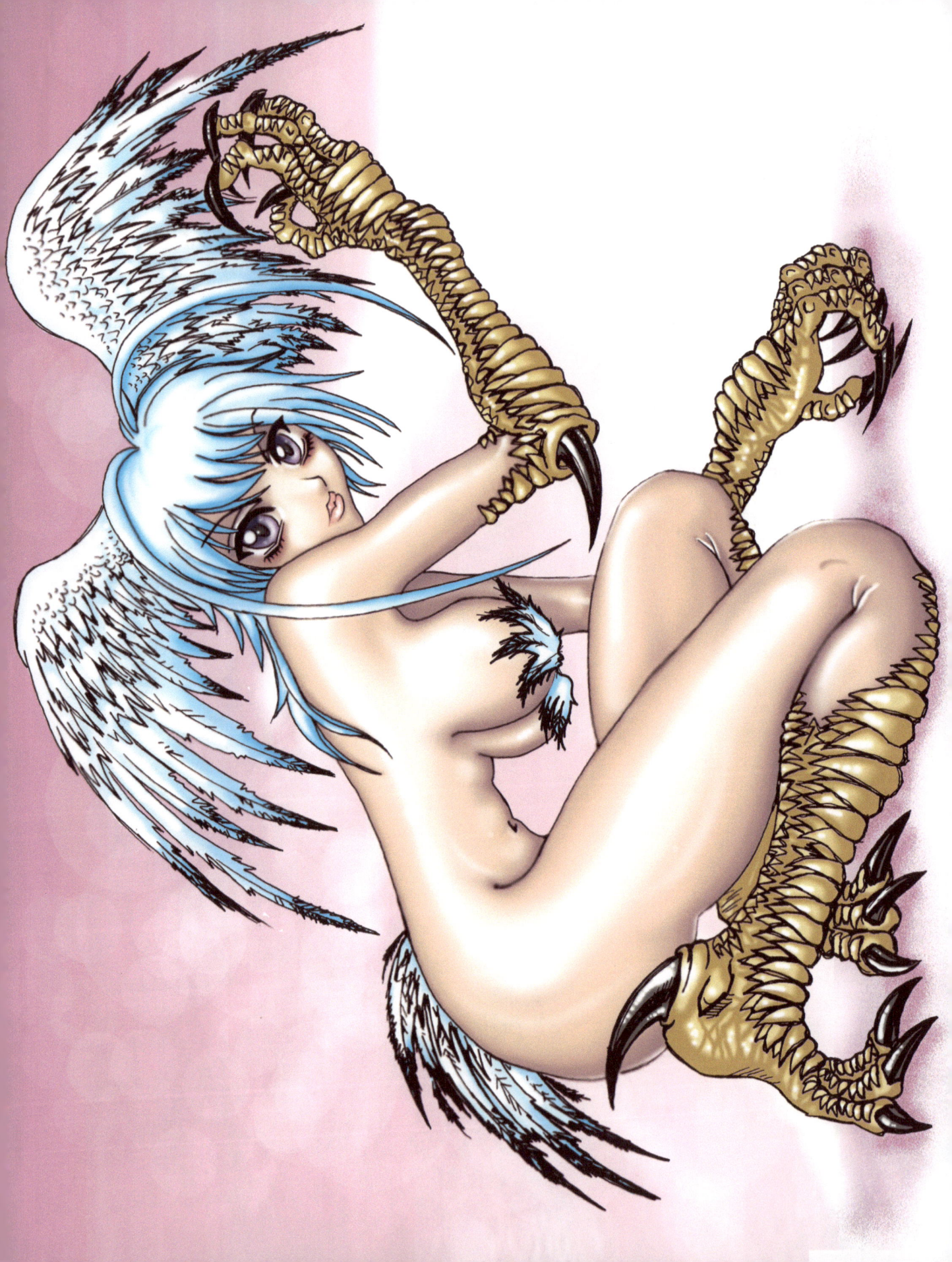

www.ingramcontent.com/pod-product-compliance
Lightning Source LLC
Chambersburg PA
CBHW050905180526
45159CB00007B/2796